THE ESSENTIAL HANDBOOK

FOR

BUSINESS WRITING

First Edition

Desmond A. Gilling

The Essential Handbook for Business Writing, First Edition.

Copyright © 2013, Desmond A. Gilling

Printed in Canada. All rights reserved.

ISBN   978-09880938-0-5

Corporate and educational quantity pricing available.

Address inquiries to: essentialbusinessenglish@gmail.com.
(011) • 1 • 416 • 400 • 8407

Printed and bound in Canada.

www.essentialbusinessenglish.com

"Good composition is like a suspension bridge—each line adds strength and takes none away." *Robert Henri*

"I have made this [letter] longer, because I have not had the time to make it shorter." *Blaise Pascal (1623–1662)*

"At painful times, when composition is impossible and reading is not enough, grammars and dictionaries are excellent for distraction."

Elizabeth Barrett Browning

"Don't use words too big for the subject. Don't say 'infinitely' when you mean 'very'; otherwise you'll have no word left when you want to talk about something really infinite."

C. S. Lewis (1898–1963)

"I try to leave out the parts that people skip."

Elmore Leonard

"One of the greatest of all faults in writing and in speaking is this: the using of many words to say little." *William Cobbett*

"I'm not a very good writer, but I'm an excellent rewriter."

James Michener

"Proofread carefully to see if you any words out."

Author Unknown

CONTENTS

COMPOSITION BASICS

BUSINESS WRITING

PROPOSALS AND REPORTS

INTRODUCTION

With the emergence of English as the official language of business worldwide, it is critical that business writers produce clear, concise communication. In business, writing tasks may range from a simple e-mail message to detailed reports and proposals; however, regardless of the simplicity or the complexity of a piece of written communication, the principles of excellent writing must be observed. Written communication is a corporate ambassador: companies will be judged by the professionalism evident in their business writing.

Because the five sections that comprise this handbook stand alone, it is not necessary to approach the text sequentially. For best results, I suggest writers begin with Composition Basics and Usage before moving forward. The Visual Basics section was included to outline the basic elements of design including font selection and page layout, which is important for those special documents that require visual enhancement.

This handbook is intended for use by all business writers, but a working knowledge of English is essential. For nonnative English speakers who have a basic level of English language proficiency, this handbook will immediately raise their writing skills level. Native English-speaking users will also benefit greatly by referring to this handbook with its simple, straightforward presentation of business writing basics and the numerous template-like writing samples. *The Essential Handbook for Business Writing* is designed to be a business writer's desktop companion.

If used as a college textbook, professors will appreciate the lesson-on-every-page format, which, if followed sequentially, provides a comprehensive Business English writing course on its own.

With this writing manual at your side, you will be able to write with confidence knowing that you are producing professionally written communication that will serve you and your business well.

Desmond A. Gilling

About The Author

Desmond Gilling is a career educator with degrees in English and Education from the University of Toronto. He has over 30 years of teaching experience including 10 years as a Business English instructor at the college level. He is a member of the Ontario College of Teachers (OCT) and of The Association For Business Communication (ABC).

Desmond currently works in the corporate sector as a copywriter and business writing instructor. His previous publications include the *EnglishSmart* language series published by Popular Books Inc.

He lives in Toronto and can be reached by e-mail at essentialbusinessenglish@gmail.com.

COMPOSITION BASICS

> "Language is the dress of thought."
> *Samuel Johnson*

In business, when you submit a piece of writing you hold yourself up to scrutiny. If your message is unclear, if your grammar is weak, if your vocabulary is imprecise, you could be judged harshly. However, if you write concisely, clearly, and with sufficient creativity to make an impact, you will be considered a highly valued asset to your company.

To write successfully you must have command of the following:

- basic grammar
- precise vocabulary
- syntax (the arrangement of words to form a sentence)
- sentence structure (the arrangement of sentence elements)
- paragraph construction

Once you've mastered the above areas, you can concentrate on creating compelling sentences and unified, coherent paragraphs.

Follow these basic rules in all correspondence:

+ Use plain English and avoid jargon.
+ Vary the length of your sentences.
+ Divide your written message into unified paragraphs.
+ Keep each paragraph to a single topic.
+ Introduce each paragraph with a strong topic sentence.
+ End each paragraph with a concluding thought.
+ Use transitional words and phrases to unify sentences and paragraphs.
+ Select the communication format that best suits your message.
+ Always use a professional tone.

The general objective of all business writing is to produce clear, concise, coherent communication.

BASIC PARTS OF SPEECH

Before building sentences, it is useful to review the basic parts of speech that make up a sentence.

Noun and Pronoun: a person, place, or thing used as the subject of either a sentence or a clause, or used as the object of a verb or preposition. A Proper Noun refers to formal names and designations.

Subjects perform action; objects receive action.

Examples:

1) The <u>manager</u> called a meeting. (subject of the sentence)
2) She asked the <u>manager</u> for assistance. (object of the verb *asked*)
3) He spoke to the <u>manager</u>. (object of the preposition *to*)
4) <u>London</u> is a European business hub. (proper noun subject)
5) The director gave <u>her</u> the job. (pronoun object of the verb *gave*)

Verb (transitive and intransitive): the action word in a sentence. A transitive verb transfers the action to an object; an intransitive verb does not require an object. (See p. 7 for more on verbs.)

Examples:

1) He <u>postponed</u> the meeting until later. (transitive with object *meeting*)
2) After the meeting, the members <u>voted</u>. (intransitive, no object)

NOTE: A verb can have either an active or a passive voice (see p.10).

Adjective: describes a noun and can be a single word or a phrase.

Examples:

1) The firm grew into a <u>profitable</u> company. (single word adjective)
2) The statement <u>on record</u> was reviewed. (adjective phrase)

Adverb: describes the action of a verb (or describes an adjective); an adverb can be a single word or a phrase.

Examples:

1) She spoke <u>clearly</u> and <u>concisely</u>. (single word adverbs)
2) She delivered her speech <u>in the boardroom</u>. (adverb phrase)
3) The message was seemingly clear, but not <u>entirely</u> understood.
(*Seemingly* describes the adjective *clear*; *entirely* describes the verb *understood*.)

BASIC PARTS OF SPEECH

Articles

The purpose of an article is to identify a noun. There are three articles: *a, an, the. A* and *an* both point to a nonspecific noun. The article *the* indicates a specific noun. Use *a* before a consonant; use *an* before a vowel and before words that begin with a mute *h*.

Examples:

1) **An** appraisal of **a** mining stock will be completed in **an** hour.
(Both the *appraisal* and the *mining stock* are nonspecific.)

2) **The** meeting was held in **the** boardroom.
(The *meeting* and the *boardroom* are specific nouns.)

Prepositions

A preposition introduces a phrase and is usually followed by a noun that is the object of the preposition.

Example:

1) He placed the files <u>in his briefcase</u>.
(The preposition *in* is followed by the object noun *briefcase*.)

Common prepositions include:

about, above, across, after, against, along, among, around, at, before, behind, below, beneath, between, beyond, down, during, for, from, in, inside, into, near, of, off, on, onto, over, past, since, through, throughout, till, to, under, underneath, until, up, upon, with, within, without.

Conjunctions

Coordinating conjunctions join elements of a sentence that have equal status: they join single words, phrases, or clauses.

Examples:

1) The president **and** the vice president will handle the formal opening **and** closing of the event, **but** they will not present awards.

2) The ideas presented were sound, **yet** not useful at this time.

3) Sales figures were low; **consequently**, the manager was fired.

NOTE: When a conjunctive adverb joins two independent clauses, it is often preceded by a semicolon and set off by a comma.

BASIC PARTS OF SPEECH

Verbals

Technically, a verbal is a derivative of a verb and not a part of speech. Verbals are important elements in constructing sentences and come in three forms: gerund, participle, and infinitive.

> **NOTE:** Misuse of a verbal can sometimes result in a sentence fragment (see p. 31).

Gerunds

A gerund is an *ing* noun-form of a verb.

Examples: (gerunds as nouns are underlined)

1) <u>Selling</u> products overseas presents a logistical problem. (subject)

2) Management encouraged <u>buying</u> updated software. (object)

Participles

Participles are either present participles or past participles, and both can be used as adjectives.

Examples: (participles as adjectives are underlined)

1) The <u>failing</u> marketing plan will be revised. (present participle)

2) She produced a <u>written</u> copy. (past participle)

Infinitives

An Infinitive is the *to* form of a verb. Infinitives can be used as nouns, adjectives, or adverbs.

Examples: (infinitives are underlined)

1) <u>To resign</u> as chairperson was her only choice. (noun/*subject*)

2) The need <u>to increase</u> profits was a priority. (adjective modifies *need*)

3) The staff worked <u>to improve</u> their skills. (adverb/modifies *worked*)

> **NOTE:** Avoid splitting an infinitive; however, at times a split infinite works for clarification or for emphasis.
> 1) She wanted <u>to boldly go</u> far afield. (acceptable)
> 2) She wanted <u>to directly fly</u> to Hong Kong. (incorrect)
> 3) She wanted <u>to fly directly</u> to Hong Kong. (correct)

composition basics

BASIC PARTS OF SPEECH
(phrases are underlined)

definite article   adjective   preposition "to"   adverb phrase

The international company relocated <u>to London</u>.

noun / subject of the sentence   proper noun / object of the preposition "to"

---

pronoun / subject   preposition "on"   semicolon joins two main clauses

She was promoted on merit; now she wanted to prove herself.

object of the preposition "on"   adverb   verb   infinitive / object

---

gerund phrase

<u>Buying stocks</u> is easy; <u>choosing a winner</u> is difficult.

gerund phrase as subject   gerund as subject

---

past participle adjective   adjective phrase   adverb phrase

A written copy <u>of the memo</u> was posted <u>on the bulletin board</u>.

noun / subject   passive verb   object of the preposition "on"

BUILDING SENTENCES: verbs

Verb Tenses: There are six verb tenses.

Simple Tenses	Perfect Tenses
present past future	present perfect past perfect future perfect

PRESENT, PAST, AND FUTURE TENSES

The **present** tense denotes present time; it may also represent consistent action or an accepted truth. The present tense can also be associated with a future idea.

The **past** tense denotes past time, and is often formed by adding *ed* to a present tense verb.

The **future** tense denotes future time and is formed by adding *shall* or *will* to a present tense verb.

Examples:

1) She <u>helps</u> the new employee with his paperwork. (*present* time)
2) She <u>works</u> in the sales department. (*present* as consistent action)
3) Hard work <u>pays off</u> in the long run. (*present* as accepted truth)
4) If we <u>work</u> hard, we will be rewarded. (*present* as future time)
5) He <u>worked</u> in the accounting department. (*past* time)
6) He <u>built</u> the company from the ground up. (*past* tense)
7) We <u>shall examine</u> the documents carefully. (*future* tense *shall*)
8) I <u>shall prepare</u> a presentation for the board. (future tense *shall*)
9) He <u>will present</u> the findings at the conference. (future tense *will*)
10) The guest speaker <u>will address</u> the group. (future tense *will*)

> **NOTE:** With first person pronouns (*I, we*), use the auxiliary *shall*. With second and third person pronouns (*you, he, she, it, they*), use the auxiliary *will*. Use *will* with all third-person subjects (see sentence 10).

TENSES: perfect and progressive

The **present perfect** tense denotes action that *has been completed* at the time of writing or action that continues into present time.

The **past perfect** tense denotes action that *was completed* before a specific time in the past.

The **future perfect** tense denotes action that *will be completed* at some specific time in the future.

Examples:

1) We <u>have formed</u> a task force. (present perfect)

2) The company <u>has built</u> a solid reputation. (present perfect)

3) She applied for the job before he <u>had learned</u> of it. (past perfect)

4) When the company folded, the employees <u>had been paid</u>. (past perfect)

5) The group <u>will have completed</u> the report at year's end. (future perfect)

6) In April, I <u>shall have worked</u> at the firm for six months. (future perfect)

PROGRESSIVE TENSES

Progressive tenses denote continued action.

Examples: (progressive forms of the six verb tenses)

1) He <u>is planning</u> to change jobs within a year. (present)

2) The assistant <u>has been calling</u> clients all day. (present perfect)

3) They <u>were considering</u> a new office location. (past)

4) She <u>had been looking</u> for work elsewhere. (past perfect)

5) The office <u>will be closing</u> for the holiday season. (future)

6) I <u>shall be working</u> in Bangkok in the new year. (future)

7) In July, they <u>will have been negotiating</u> for a year. (future perfect)

8) They <u>are going to restructure</u> the company. (future using *going*)

THE MOOD OF A VERB

The mood of a verb indicates whether a writer is expressing a statement, a command, a wish, or a recommendation. There are three moods: **indicative**, **imperative**, and **subjunctive**.

The **Indicative Mood** indicates a fact or question.

    1) The company <u>builds</u> computer components.

    2) Where does the company <u>ship</u> its computer parts?

The **Imperative Mood** indicates a command.

    1) <u>Don't underestimate</u> your competition.

    2) When the alarm sounds, <u>leave</u> the building immediately.

The **Subjunctive Mood** indicates conditions, recommendations, or wishes that are contrary to fact; the subjunctive mood is most often used in formal rather than casual writing. (Note the use of plural verbs with singular subjects to create the subjunctive mood.)

    1) <u>If</u> the facility <u>were</u> larger, more product could be made. (not *was*)

    2) She wished she <u>were</u> in a position of power. (not *was*)

    3) <u>Should</u> the facts <u>be</u> true, the outlook is grim. (not *if* and *are*)

    4) If he had had better training, he would be a manager. (not *had*)

PROBLEM VERBS

    lie / lay   sit / set   rise / raise

Examples:

    1) He <u>lied</u> about his past business dealings.

    2) Every day, on her break, she <u>lies</u> down for an hour.

    3) The files <u>are lying</u> on the desk. (not laying)

    4) The files <u>have lain</u> on the desk for over a week. (not have laid)

    5) The committee members will <u>sit</u> in their assigned chairs.

    6) The files were <u>set</u> in front of the committee members. (placed)

    7) The rules for the debate were <u>set</u> in stone. (idiomatic)

    8) The price of oil will continue to <u>rise</u>.

    9) She has <u>risen</u> quickly into the ranks of management.

    10) The supplier <u>raised</u> the price of product delivery.

    11) She <u>will raise</u> her voice to make her point.

VERBS: Active and Passive Voice

In the **active** voice the subject performs the action.

> The company president delivered a speech.
> (subject)　(verb)　(object)

In the **passive** voice the subject receives the action.

> The speech was delivered by the company president.
> (subject)　(verb)

The active voice is usually preferred over the passive voice. The active voice is more forceful and direct; the passive voice might suggest indifference or a lack of responsibility of the performer of the action (verb). However, if the subject of the verb is unknown or of less importance than the action itself, the passive voice works well.

In these examples the passive voice is awkward.

Active Voice:　He remembers his university days fondly.

Passive Voice:　His university days are fondly remembered by him.

Active Voice:　She examined the files for inconsistencies.

Passive Voice:　The files were examined by her for inconsistencies.

In this example the passive voice creates ambiguity.

Passive Voice:　He was impressed with the director—he was thorough.

(To whom does the second *he*, after the dash, refer?)

In this example the passive voice is unambiguous.

Passive Voice:　He was impressed with the director who was thorough.

(No ambiguity: *director* is the antecedent of *who*.)

Active Voice:　The director who was thorough impressed him.

In the next two examples the passive voice is preferred.

Passive Voice:　The meetings were put on hold.

(Passive voice used with unknown subject.)

Passive Voice:　The executive was given the CEO of the Year Award.

(Passive voice puts emphasis on receiver of the action.)

NOTE: The passive voice is often preferred in technical or scientific writing where the process described is more important than the subject of the action.

SUBJECT-VERB AGREEMENT

A verb must agree with its governing noun in both number and person.

number = singular or plural subject

person = first, second, or third

Examples:

1) I am **delivering** a speech at the meeting. (first person singular)

2) You **are** responsible for the agenda. (second person singular)

3) Alex **works** in the accounting department. (third person singular)

4) We usually **design** the newsletter together. (first person plural)

5) John and Craig **act** as consultants. (third person compound)

To create a third person plural subject add either *s* or *es*. To create a singular verb add *s* or *es*.

6) **Photocopiers** need regular maintenance. (plural subject – *s*)

7) A photocopier **needs** regular maintenance. (singular verb – *s*)

8) The manager **goes** overseas annually. (singular verb – *es*)

Exceptions: the verbs *have* and *be*

9) I **have** business in the city. (first person singular subject with *have*)

10) We **have** business in the city. (first person plural subject with *have*)

11) I **have** a business degree; he **has** a science degree. (singular verbs)

12) I **am** an accountant and he **is** a lawyer. (singular forms of *be*)

When the subject and verb are separated by words or phrases, it is easy to misinterpret which subject governs the verb.

Examples: (the crossed-out verbs below would be governed by the wrong noun)

1) The <u>minutes</u> of the meeting ~~is~~ **are** posted on the website.

2) The <u>CEO</u>, one of the board members, ~~agree~~ **agrees** with the policy.

3) The <u>manager</u> and the <u>employees</u> ~~discusses~~ **discuss** a salary increase.

NOTE: Linking Verbs are governed by their subject not by the complement.

1) His <u>concern</u> **is** employees who are frequently absent. (singular)

2) <u>Employees</u> who **are** frequently absent are his main concern. (plural)

SUBJECT–VERB AGREEMENT

COMPOUND SUBJECTS

When two subjects are joined by a conjunction they require a plural verb. However, if a compound subject is considered to be a single unit, a singular verb is used.

Examples: plural compound subjects

1) Ahmad and Gupreet **are** co-convening the meeting.

2) Creativity, hard work, and planning **are** critical to success.

But: compounds as single units

3) <u>The lost and found</u> **is** located at the front desk. (singular verb)

4) <u>Bacon and eggs</u> was served at the meeting. (singular verb)

Each and Every

When the term *each* or *every* precedes subjects joined by *and*, the verb is singular.

5) *Each* written <u>report</u> and <u>proposal</u> **adheres** to a specific format.

6) *Each* <u>manager</u> and *every* <u>employee</u> **is** having an evaluation.

7) *Every* <u>manufacturer</u> and *every* <u>distributor</u> **is** hired on contract.

Or and Nor

When a compound subject is joined by the term *or* or *nor*, the verb agrees in number with the closest subject.

8) *Neither* the president *nor* the <u>managers</u> **are** available. (plural verb)

9) *Neither* the facts n*or* her <u>interpretation</u> **is** useful. (singular verb)

COLLECTIVE NOUNS

Collective nouns usually represent a group but are singular or plural in form depending on the context or meaning.

Examples:

1) The <u>staff</u> **is** working overtime to finish the project. (single unit)

2) The marketing <u>staff</u> **are** arriving at different times. (plural unit)

NOTE: In example (1) "staff" is a collective single unit.
In example (2) "staff" refers to a group of individual staff members.
To avoid the awkwardness of a plural verb with a collective noun, add a defining phrase: for clarification add "a member of..." to examples (1) and "the members of..." to example (2).

PRONOUNS

TYPES OF PRONOUNS

Reflexive pronouns (*himself, herself, myself, itself, yourself, ourselves, themselves*) refer to their antecedent nouns.

1) The investor impressed *himself* with his market predictions.

2) After the Stock Market drop, the analyst did not seem *herself.*

Intensive pronouns (*himself, herself, myself, itself, yourself, ourselves, themselves*) add emphasis to an antecedent.

1) He *himself* was surprised at the hostile takeover.

2) The analyst wasn't comfortable *herself* with the investments.

Demonstrative pronouns (*this, that, these, those*) indicate specific nouns.

1) *This* show of support by management was encouraging.

2) *Those* employees who work overtime will be compensated.

Interrogative pronouns ask *who, which,* or *what.*

1) *Who* will lead the discussion?

2) *Which* venue is best suited for the meeting?

3) *What* is the main topic for discussion?

Reciprocal pronouns (*each other, one another*) refer to individual segments of a plural antecedent.

1) The two managers disagreed with *each other* over staffing needs.

2) After the meeting they shook hands with *one another.*

Indefinite pronouns (*all, any, both, each, either, everybody, none, one, several, some, somebody, someone*) do not refer to a specific person or thing. An indefinite pronoun may also be an adjective.

1) *Both* of them completed a degree in commerce. (noun)

2) *Both* students completed a degree in commerce. (adjective)

3) *Anyone* willing to work hard can succeed. (noun)

4) *Each* employee has an opinion. (noun)

NOTE: The pronouns *who, whom, whoever,* and *whomever* refer to people; the pronouns *what, that, whatever,* and *whichever* refer to things. *Whose* can refer to either people or things.

RELATIVE PRONOUNS: who, whom, whoever, whomever

Choosing which of these terms to use is problematic because there is the issue of grammatical correctness as opposed to familiar usage.

To some, the object case (*whom* or *whomever*) is archaic; consequently, this usage is slowly being eliminated from spoken language. Simply put, *whom* and *whomever* do not always roll off the tongue easily.

Examples:

Whom did you report to in the overseas office? (formal)

in contrast to

Who did you report to in the foreign office? (casual)

To solve this dilemma assume a compromise. When composing business correspondence be formal and grammatically correct: **who** as a subject and **whom** as an object. When speaking, which is often less formal than writing, use the term most natural to your tone.

Examples:

1) Who will you get legal advice from regarding the dispute? (casual)

2) From whom will you get legal advice regarding the dispute?

In the above examples, sentence (2) is grammatically correct, but sentence (1) might be preferred orally, particularly in casual conversation.

3) The new president is not whom The Board preferred. (correct)

4) The new president is who will make changes in policy. (correct)

In sentence (3) *whom* is object of the verb *preferred*; in sentence (4) *who* is subject of the verb *will make*.

And

5) He assigned the task to **whoever** was capable.

6) He assigned the task to **whomever** he thought suitable.

In sentence (5) *whoever* is the subject of the verb *was capable*; in sentence (6) *whomever* is object of the preposition *to*.

RELATIVE PRONOUNS: that, which

Relative pronouns are *relative* because they relate to a noun antecedent that usually appears earlier in a sentence.

> **That** is a *restrictive* (defining) pronoun.
>
> **Which** is a *nonrestrictive* pronoun.

Examples:

1) The laptop **that** needs repairing is at the front desk.

(The *restrictive* clause beginning with *that* relates to its antecedent the laptop distinguishing it as the <u>only</u> laptop at the front desk.)

2) One of the laptops, **which** she often uses, is in need of repair.

(The *nonrestrictive* clause beginning with *which* merely offers additional information about one of the laptops she uses.)

3) She was told to review accounts **that** have overdue invoices.

(The *restrictive* clause beginning with *that* refers to specific *accounts*)

4) The accounts, **which** are in brown folders, have overdue invoices.

(The *nonrestrictive* clause beginning with *which* offers additional information about the accounts, but the main fact is that these accounts are overdue.)

AMBIGUITY

If the pronouns **that** and **which** are not placed directly after or close to an antecedent, ambiguity occurs.

Examples:

1) She has prepared a presentation on global trade, **which** has become a problem.

(Unclear: Does *which* refer to the *presentation* or to *global trade?*)

2) The presentation **that** she has prepared on global trade has become a problem.

(Clear: *that* refers to its antecedent *presentation.*)

3) She worked all night on the information for the conference **that** was necessary.

(Unclear: Does *that* refer to *information* or to *conference?*)

4) She worked all night on the information **that** was necessary for the conference.

(Clear: *that* refers to its antecedent *information.*)

PRONOUN CONFUSION: than *I*, than *me*, as *I*, as *me*

The words *than* and *as* are either conjunctions or prepositions—a distinction that is critical to the meaning of a sentence. As prepositions they would be followed by an object pronoun; as conjunctions they would be followed by a subject pronoun.

> **NOTE:** The choice of object or subject pronoun can alter the meaning of the sentence.

Examples: (two different meanings)

1) She likes sales more than **me**. (compares *me* to *sales*)
2) She likes sales more than **I**. (than I *like sales*)

In example (1) *than* is followed by the object pronoun *me*, which might seem correct when spoken, but is faulty. The problem is that the object pronoun suggests a direct comparison between *me* and *sales*. Reversing the sentence to "She likes *me* more than *sales*" illustrates the nonsensical comparison of *sales* to *me*. Sentence (2) makes more sense as it means that *she likes sales more than I do.*

> **NOTE:** When in doubt, test that the sentence makes sense by adding the "understood" words before choosing the pronoun.

Examples: (two different meanings)

3) Management relied on *me* more than *him*. (comparison)
4) Management relied on *me* more than *he*. (than *he* relied on *me*)

In sentence (3) the comparison of *me* to *him* is obvious. In sentence (4) add the word *did* after *he* to avoid confusion: "Management relied on me more than *he did.*"

Examples: (two different meanings)

5) I enjoy working with *her* as well as *him*. (working with *him* also)
6) I enjoy working with *her* as well as *he*. (as well as *he* does)
7) He doesn't work as hard as ~~me~~ I do.

In sentence (5) the subject enjoyed working with both *her* and *him*. In sentence (6) both *I* and *he* are subjects of the verb *enjoyed* and both enjoyed working with *her*. In sentence (7), the objective case (me) is clearly incorrect if the verb *do* is included.

PRONOUN-ANTECEDENT AGREEMENT

A pronoun is relevant when representing a noun antecedent. Ambiguity occurs when the antecedent of the pronoun is unclear.

(In the sentences below the antecedents are underlined.)

When the <u>accountant</u> submitted **his** report, **he** met the deadline.

After the <u>managers</u> submitted **their** reports, **they** waited for a decision.

AGREEMENT WITH NUMBER AND GENDER:

1) <u>Consultants</u> offer training to **their** clients. (plural)

2) A <u>lawyer</u> defends **his** or **her** client. (mixed gender)

3) <u>Each</u> of the corporations had **its** plan for a takeover. (singular)

GENDER:

1) At the meeting, <u>Mr. Alvarez</u> outlined **his** plan for new business.

2) <u>Ms. Sanchez</u> created the new logo that **she** unveiled today.

3) <u>Mr. Rhuen</u> and <u>Ms. Singh</u> each submitted **his** and **her** expenses.

4) <u>Ms. Chu</u> and <u>Ms. Lau</u> presented **their** marketing analysis.

5) Fifteen <u>staff members</u> attended the conference. **Each** handed in her or his evaluation to the department manager.

(In the past, the masculine would be used with mixed genders; today, it is more appropriate to use the phrases *him* or *her*, *hers* or *his*, or *she* or *he*.)

COLLECTIVE NOUN ANTECEDENT

If the members of a group (collective noun antecedent) are treated individually, use a plural pronoun. Use a singular pronoun if the antecedent collective noun is treated as a single unit.

Examples:

1) The director asked the sales <u>team</u> to produce **their** results.
(Each member of the sales team is to produce **his** and **her** results.)

2) The board allowed the <u>firm</u> to hit **its** lowest valuation.
(The firm is a single unit.)

3) The <u>marketing group</u> prepared **its** strategy for next year.
(The marketing group is a single unit.)

PRONOUN-VERB AGREEMENT

Indefinite pronouns are nonspecific and can be either singular or plural. This presents a problem because they may sound plural, but could be grammatically singular.

SINGULAR INDEFINITE PRONOUNS: use singular verb

Singular Indefinite Pronouns

another	everyone	nothing
anybody	everything	one
anyone	much	other
anything	neither	somebody
each	nobody	someone
either	no one	something

Examples:

1) Everyone on staff **is** attending a training seminar.

2) Each of the proposals **has** merit.

3) Neither of the clients **was** happy with the service they received.

4) Of the two proposals, neither **is** acceptable.

INDEFINITE PRONOUNS: singular and plural verbs

Plural Verb Only		Singular or Plural Verb	
both	others	all	most
few	several	any	none
many		more	some

Examples:

1) Of the candidates that applied, several **are** qualified. (plural verb)

2) All of these candidates **show** promise. (plural verb)

3) All the planning for the interviews **is** complete. (singular verb)

4) Most of the discussion **was** about compensation. (singular verb)

RELATIVE PRONOUN SUBJECTS

When a relative pronoun—*who, which,* or *that*—is the subject of a verb, that verb must agree in number with the antecedent of the pronoun.

Examples:

1) Hard work is an <u>ingredient</u> **that** ensures success.
(*That* refers to *ingredient* and therefore takes a singular verb.)

2) The <u>advisors</u> **who** were hired as consultants created solutions.
(*Who* refers to *advisors* and therefore takes a plural verb.)

3) A <u>copy</u> of the files, **which** is stored securely, **is** now available.
(*Which* refers to *copy* not to *files* and takes a singular verb.)

When the term "one of" comes before a relative pronoun, be careful to make the correct association of subject and verb.

Examples:

1) Sarah is <u>one</u> of the staff who **work** on weekends.
(Plural: the meaning is that Sarah is not <u>the only</u> staff member working.)

2) Sarah is the only <u>one</u> of the staff who **works** on weekends.)
(Singular: Sarah is <u>the only</u> staff member working.)

LINKING VERBS

A verb should agree with the subject that precedes it, not with the complementary subject that follows. (The subjects are underlined.)

1) The <u>writing</u> of proposals ~~were~~ **is** the reason for working late.

2) The <u>ideas</u> of the group ~~is~~ **are** the key to formulating a plan.

Some nouns appear plural but could be singular, depending on context.

Examples:

1) <u>Statistics</u> **involves** the study of numerical analysis. (singular)

2) The <u>statistics</u> in the report **indicate** an in-depth study. (plural)

If the title of a work of art is plural, it takes a singular verb.

3) *The Essentials* is a business book published by Harvard Press.

The verb must also agree with its subject that follows.

4) In the back room ~~is~~ **are** the filing <u>cabinets</u>. (subject: cabinets)

Some inverted (verb-subject) sentences begin with "there" followed by a form of the verb *to be.* The term "there" is never a subject.

5) There **are** three separate <u>offices</u> on each floor. (plural verb)

6) There **is** one main <u>reason</u> to expand: profits. (singular verb)

VAGUE PRONOUN REFERENCES

Create clear pronoun-antecedent associations. Avoid applying a pronoun to represent an entire idea in a sentence or to represent a vague antecedent.

Vague:

> The salesperson spent time learning the product, researching marketing data, and creating a target client list, **which** proved to be good planning.

(*Which* should refer to all the action in the sentence, not just the final element)

Clear:

> The salesperson exercised good planning by learning the product, researching market data, and creating a target client list.

Vague:

> Department managers should delegate responsibility and monitor activity closely. **This** is important for productivity.

(Does *this* refer to *delegating* or to *monitoring?*)

Clear:

> For productivity, it is important that managers delegate responsibility and monitor activity.

AMBIGUOUS PRONOUN REFERENCE

Avoid using a pronoun that could refer to more than one antecedent.

Unclear:

> Mr. Sen told Mr. Liu that **he** would be reassigned.

(There is no way of knowing which person is being reassigned.)

Clear:

> Mr. Sen told Mr Liu, "**You** are being reassigned."
>
> Mr. Sen announced the reassignment of Mr. Liu.

Unclear:

> The sales campaign will begin with a product launch. **It** will last three months.

(Does *it* refer to the *campaign* or to the *launch?*)

Clear:

> The three-month sales campaign will begin with a product launch.

More on Pronoun Usage

A pronoun should not immediately follow its antecedent.

1) The accountant ~~he~~ knows the true financial picture.
2) The government workers ~~they~~ will go on strike next Monday.

Use pronouns *myself*, *himself*, *herself*, and *themselves* only when the antecedent appears in the sentence.

1) <u>I</u> arranged the meeting for Mr. Tanaka and **myself**. (not *and me*)
2) The reports were given to Ms. Chanda and ~~myself~~ me. (use *me*)
3) <u>They</u> **themselves** felt responsible for the downturn in profits.
4) <u>Mr. Desjardin</u> and <u>Ms. Chen</u> bought iPads for **themselves**.

The cases of a pronoun depend on its use in a sentence.

subjective	objective	possessive
I you he she it we they who whomever	me you him her it us them whom whomever	my mine your yours his her hers its our ours their theirs whose

Compound Subjects and Objects

1) Paul and ~~me~~ I have worked together for many years. (subject)
2) Neither the CEO nor ~~him~~ he wants to make the decision. (subject)
3) The award was given to both Leonard and ~~I~~ me. (object)
4) Invite Susan and ~~she~~ her to the reception. (object)

With Appositive Construction

1) The board members—Singh, Smith, and ~~me~~ I—will confer.
2) Two employees—Harry and ~~her~~ she—applied for a raise this year.

Subjective Case for Predicate Nominative

1) The people to see for clarification are Joanne and ~~her~~ she. (subject)

Before Verbals

1) The client did not agree with ~~she~~ her writing the report.
2) She remembered ~~his~~ him smiling when talking to the clients.

TYPES OF SENTENCES

There are four basic types of sentences: simple, compound, complex, and compound-complex. Make your business message more engaging by using these sentence types to create variety.
(See the section on clauses, pages 24–27.)

THE SIMPLE SENTENCE (also referred to as an independent clause)

The *simple sentence* conveys one main idea consisting of the following: a subject (performer of the action), a verb (the action), descriptors (adverbs and adjectives), and, in some cases, an object (receiver of the action).

Example:

The accounting department will conduct a detailed audit.

subject: accounting department   **verb:** will conduct

object: audit   **adjective:** detailed

THE COMPOUND SENTENCE

The *compound sentence* consists of two *independent* but related clauses.

Examples: (conjunctions joining independent clauses are in bold)

1) Sales are up this year at the European office **and** the marketing staff from that region will receive a bonus.

2) The main plant will be hiring this spring, **but** it is not yet known how many new positions will be offered.

THE COMPLEX SENTENCE

The *complex sentence* consists of one independent clause and one or more dependent clauses.

Example: (dependent clause in italics cannot stand alone)

Although there was disagreement, a consensus was reached.

(When a dependent clause appears first, it is usually followed by a comma.)

Example: (independent clause in italics can stand alone)

Investment in foreign countries can be very profitable even though there may be a margin of risk.

(When an independent clause appears first, a comma is not needed.)

NOTE: Terminology
independent clause = simple sentence (stands alone)
dependent clause   = subordinate clause (cannot stand alone)

THE COMPOUND-COMPLEX SENTENCE

The compound-complex sentence consists of two or more independent clauses and at least one dependent clause.

Examples: (dependent clauses in italics)

1) *Although it will be costly at first,* expansion into global markets is necessary **and** the firm will investigate this option.

2) Employees will be moved to the fifth floor **and** they will share workspace *because their regular office is under renovation.*

The following paragraph contains the basic types of sentences.

Sentence (1) is simple.   Sentence (2) is complex.

Sentence (3) is compound.   Sentence (4) is compound-complex.

(1) The decision of the board of directors regarding expansion to North America was pending further investigation. (2) Although the facts originally presented seemed conclusive, there was concern that costs were too high. (3) However, cost was not all that was standing in the way of a final decision and the board knew this. (4) Even though the expansion needed to be initiated in a timely fashion, the board of directors decided to hire a consulting firm to do a feasibility study and they will discuss the findings with North American affiliates.

CONSIDERATION FOR YOUR READER

+ Use a variety of sentences: simple, compound, complex, compound-complex.
+ Vary the length of sentences.
+ Use long sentences to keep related information together.
+ Use short sentences for emphasis and to provide relief for the reader.
+ Use short sentences to highlight a key point.
+ Introduce your paragraph with a strong topic sentence.
+ Be clear, concise, and grammatically correct.

"Have something to say, and say it as clearly as you can. That is the only secret."
Mathew Arnold

PHRASES AND CLAUSES

PHRASES

Phrases and clauses are integral to forming clear, well-constructed sentences. A clause in a sentence allows the writer to accentuate key ideas by altering the order in which these ideas are presented.

The simple difference between a phrase and a clause is that a phrase does not contain a subject and a verb, while a clause contains both. There are two kinds of phrases: **prepositional** and **verbal**.

Prepositional Phrases

Prepositional phrases begin with prepositions such as *in, at, on, from, to, after, before, during,* and are followed by a noun. Generally, prepositional phrases answer the questions *where, when,* or *how* (adverbs) or *what* (adjectives).

Examples: (prepositional phrases)

1) She invited questions *during the presentation.* (adverb phrase)

2) The work *of the panel* resulted in policy change. (adjective phrase)

Verbal Phrases

There are three kinds of verbal phrases: participle, gerund, and infinitive. The **gerund phrase** takes on the role of a noun acting as a subject or object in a sentence; the **participle phrase** acts as an adjective; the **infinitive phrase** can act as a noun, adjective, or adverb.

Examples: (gerund phrases in italics)

1) *Hiring new staff* is necessary for business growth. (noun/subject)

2) She preferred *allocating work* to *doing it herself.* (nouns/objects)

Examples: (participle phrases in italics)

1) The clerk *working late* was alone in the office. (adjective)

2) She reviewed the details *outlined in the office memo.* (adjective)

Examples: (infinitive phrases in italics; infinitives underlined)

1) <u>To solve</u> *a problem* can be satisfying and rewarding. (noun)

2) Professional training is one way <u>to advance</u> *in business.* (adjective)

3) She was delighted <u>to serve</u> *on the board of directors.* (adverb)

CLAUSES

A clause contains both a subject and a verb and can be either independent or dependent. An independent clause is a simple sentence expressing a complete thought; a dependent clause, although expressing a thought, cannot stand on its own.

Examples: (dependent clauses underlined)

1) <u>When they take a trip</u>, they fly business class.

2) She prepared the paperwork <u>before she met with the client</u>.

In each example above, the dependent clause (underlined) contains a subject and a verb, but does not stand alone: each requires the main clause in the sentence to make the statement complete. There are three types of dependent clauses: adverb, adjective, and noun.

The **Adverb Clause** usually begins with a subordinating conjunction (see note below) and acts as an adverb modifying the verb.

Examples: (verbs underlined; modifying adverb clauses in italics)

1) The company <u>experienced</u> exponential growth *after it developed a new product line.*

2) *Although production expanded,* the company <u>did not hire</u> new staff.

The **Adjective Clause**, also known as a relative clause, modifies a noun or pronoun.

Examples: (noun and noun phrases underlined; adjective clause in italics)

1) <u>The new CEO</u>, *who is from Hong Kong*, has made several changes.

2) <u>PowerPoint</u>, *which is overused*, is not always effective.

3) <u>The office building</u> *where she works* is on Wall Street.

A **Noun Clause** acts as a noun in a sentence.

Examples: (noun clauses in italics)

1) *That she left the company* was a surprise to everyone. (subject)

2) The seminar dealt with *why the economy is stalled*. (object)

> **NOTE:** A **subordinating conjunction** links a dependent clause to an independent clause. Subordinating conjunctions include: *after, although, as, because, before, even though, if, since....*

RESTRICTIVE AND NONRESTRICTIVE CLAUSES AND PHRASES

A **restrictive** clause or phrase adds necessary information to a sentence; a **nonrestrictive** clause or phrase adds information that is not necessary to the main idea of the sentence but adds detail.

> NOTE: No comma is necessary to set off a *restrictive* clause or phrase. However, place a comma before and after a *nonrestrictive* clause or phrase.

Examples: (restrictive clauses and phrases in italics)

1) The new appointee *who is a specialist in forensic accounting* will report for work one week from today. (necessary information)

2) The committee members *although previously in disagreement* were able to reach a consensus. (necessary information)

Examples: (nonrestrictive clauses and phrases, commas used)

1) The new appointee, *a graduate of the London Business School,* will report for work one week from today. (extra information)

2) The committee members, *although chosen at random,* agreed with the mandate. (extra information)

> NOTE: Commas or dashes are used to set off a parenthetical element that acts as a parallel to another term in a sentence.

COMMA USE WITH A PARENTHETICAL CONSTRUCTION

In the parenthetical construction (example (1) below) *the new building* and *the South Tower* are the same reference. In example (2), *Singapore* and *one* are the same reference.

Examples:

1) The offices in new building, *the South Tower,* are more convenient than those in the former location.

2) Singapore—*one of the world's major financial hubs*—is home to numerous international banks.

PHRASES AND CLAUSES IN SENTENCES

Not only do phrases and clauses add information to a sentence, they provide an opportunity for the writer to alter the presentation of ideas. Also, the combination of sentence types (simple, compound, complex, compound-complex) within a paragraph is pleasing to the reader.

Simple Sentences

noun phrase

The <u>Board of Directors</u> made the final decision. All department managers received copies <u>of the documents</u>.

adjective phrase

Compound Sentence

adjective phrase

Most employees <u>of the bank</u> preferred to take long weekends *in the summer,* but some chose regular <u>holiday time</u>.

adverb phrase

noun phrase

Complex Sentences

dependent clauses   independent clause

While he was driving to work, *he listened to an audio book.*
(comma above)   Independent clause

The plane arrived late because the weather was bad.
(no comma above)

Compound-Complex Sentences

dependent clauses

Although the stock market is currently underperforming, *investments in Resources remain brisk* and *the outlook for this sector is positive.*

Before the annual report is published and before the committee examines its contents, *the directors will do a final review.*

independent clauses

NOTE: A dependent clause appearing first in a sentence is separated from the independent clause by a comma; however, if the dependent clause is short, a comma separating the clauses is not necessary.

CONSTRUCTING SENTENCES

Business writers should be aware that when creating a document there are many options for constructing sentences and developing unified and coherent paragraphs. A simple sentence may be all that is needed to convey a single idea; a more complex sentence may be required to transmit more detailed information. Varying the types of sentences ensures that emphasis will be properly placed and that the purpose of the message will be clear to the reader.

NOTE: A simple sentence is also referred to as an independent clause.

To compose effective sentences, consider the following:

- choice of words: plain, direct language is vital for clarity and tone
- types of sentences (simple, compound, complex, compound-complex): these must suit both content and purpose
- strategic order of sentence parts: clarity and emphasis attained
- punctuation: the comma, colon, semicolon, and the dash have a function in strategically arranging and presenting sentence parts

SENTENCE COMBINING: a strategy for creating sentences

- Short sentences covering a common topic can be combined various ways (see p. 30). Phrases and clauses within a sentence can be arranged strategically to best present information.

- Short sentences can be joined by a conjunction, a semicolon, a colon, a dash, or by making one sentence dependent on the other (dependent and independent clauses).

- A dependent clause may be placed first in a sentence to qualify the independent clause that follows. When the main idea is most important, place it first followed by the dependent clause that gives supportive details.

- Phrases should always be positioned close to the word they modify. An adjective phrase should be next to its noun; an adverb phrase should be close to its verb.

CONSTRUCTING SENTENCES

In business writing, the **semicolon** should be used sparingly. However, when there are two closely related sentences of equal weight and the writer wants a tight, efficient construction, a semicolon works well.

The board meeting came to an abrupt close; none of the major issues were resolved.

In the above sentence, the *closing* and the unresolved *issues* are closely related. By combining these sentences with a semicolon, the writer is direct and emphatic.

A **colon** is used when the statement that follows completes the initial thought.

The corporation had one focus: expansion worldwide.

The statement following the colon is abrupt and emphatic. The two words *expansion worldwide* bring a forceful completion to the sentence.

The corporation's main focus was expansion worldwide.

Although the sentence above is stating the same thing as the second sentence, the impact is not as strong. However, in business writing, excessively dramatic endings are best avoided.

ARRANGING CLAUSES

A **dependent clause** appearing first in a sentence will introduce or qualify the main idea to follow; it may also ease the reader into the message.

Because of a slow economy and a shrinking market share, the company will be considering a reduction in operations.

The **dependent clause** (because of a...share) appears first to buffer the news of a possible *reduction in operations*. Before the bad news is given, the opening dependent clause acts as a qualifier.

The plant will be closed within a month because of a slowdown in production.

Above, the **main clause** comes first while the dependent clause that follows adds an explanation.

CONSTRUCTING SENTENCES

Here are two simple sentences that are combined five ways.

(a) The sales staff worked very hard.

(b) The sales staff exceeded their quota.

The sales staff worked very hard and they exceeded their quota.
(The sentences are joined by a conjunction.)

The sales staff worked very hard; they exceeded their quota.
(The sentences are joined by a semicolon.)

The sales staff exceeded their quota: the result of hard work.
(A completing thought follows the colon.)

The sales staff exceeded their quota—a result of their hard work.
(The statement following the dash refers to the initial idea.)

Because they worked very hard, the sales staff exceeded their quota.
Sentence (a) is a dependent clause introducing the main clause.)

Here are three short sentences combined using three methods.

(a) She is now director of Asian operations.

(b) She is a solid performer in the Asian office.

(c) The position demands extensive travel.

Because she is a solid performer in the Asian office, she is now director of Asian operations: a position demanding extensive travel.
(Sentence (b) is dependent; sentence (c) becomes the completing thought.)

She is now director of Asian operations because she is a solid performer in that region. This position demands extensive travel.
(The statements above consist of a complex sentence and a simple sentence.)

As director of operations for Asia—a promotion received because of her solid performance in that region—she will travel extensively.
(Sentence (b) is parenthetic.)

NOTE: As evident in the examples above, there are many choices when constructing sentences. Convey the desired affect of the message, but always be clear and concise.

FAULTY SENTENCE STRUCTURE

Faulty sentence structure is intolerable in business writing. To avoid structural errors, it is important to have a thorough knowledge of the following major errors:

1) comma splice 2) sentence fragment 3) fused or run-on sentence

SENTENCE FRAGMENT

A sentence fragment is not a sentence because it either lacks a subject or a verb, or it is a dependent clause that requires the support of an independent clause. A dependent clause may contain a complete thought, but is not structurally a complete sentence.

Examples:

Fragment: Whenever there is spare time to read.
(A dependent clause is incorrectly used as a sentence.)

Correct: Whenever there is spare time to read, she enjoys fiction.
(An independent clause is added making the sentence complete.)

Fragment: Worked late into the night.
(The subject is missing.)

Correct: The sales staff worked late into the night.
(The subject "sales staff" is added.)

Fragment: Consultants from overseas meeting at the conference.
(The word "meeting" is a verbal, not a verb.)

Correct: Consultants from overseas are meeting at the conference.
(The verb "are meeting" is added.)

Fragment: Although leaving late. We arrived at the meeting on time.
(The verbal "leaving" is used in place of a verb creating a fragment.)

Correct: Although we left late, we arrived at the meeting on time.
(The fragment becomes a dependent clause.)

NOTE: Sentence fragments are sometimes used for emphasis. In advertising copy, for example, the statement "Simply The Best" is a fragment intended to highlight a selling point. A fragment is never acceptable in business writing. A fragment appearing in a document undermines the credibility of the writer.

COMMA SPLICE

A comma splice occurs when a comma is used to separate two independent clauses; however, if the independent clauses are short and closely related, a comma may be used (see Note below).

A comma splice can be corrected in the following ways:

1) Replace the comma with a coordinating conjunction (*and, but, whereas, therefore, although, etc.*).

2) Join closely related ideas with a semicolon.

3) Form separate sentences.

4) Make one clause dependent on the other.

Examples:

Incorrect: The company is expanding rapidly, their product is now sold worldwide. (comma creates a splice)

Correct: The company is expanding rapidly and their product is now sold worldwide. (joined by the conjunction *and*)

Correct: The company is expanding rapidly; their product is now sold worldwide. (joined by a semicolon)

Correct: The company is expanding rapidly. Their product is now sold worldwide. (two sentences formed)

Correct: Because their product is now sold worldwide, the company is expanding rapidly. (dependent clause set off by a comma)

NOTE: If two independent clauses are short and closely related in content, they may be joined by a comma. Although this structure may have a dramatic effect and is technically acceptable, it is usually best avoided.

Correct: He does the page design, she does the writing.
Correct: The stock value goes up, the investors are happy.

FUSED AND RUN-ON SENTENCES

A fused sentence occurs when two independent clauses are joined without punctuation or a conjunction separating them. In essence, a fused sentence is a comma splice without the comma. A run-on sentence is simply a lengthy fused sentence.

A fused sentence and a comma splice can be corrected the same ways:

1) Use a coordinating conjunction (*and*, *but*...); or, insert *and* after inserting a comma.

2) Separate the two independent statements with a semicolon.

3) Form separate sentences.

4) Make one clause dependent on the other.

Example: (the problem area is underlined)

Fused: The stock market <u>declined investors</u> were worried.

Correct: The stock market declined and investors were worried.

Correct: The stock market declined; investors were worried.

Correct: The stock market declined. Investors were worried.

Correct: Because the stock market declined, investors were worried.

Run-on: Make a summary of the <u>meeting send</u> a copy to all <u>departments have</u> the managers forward their comments.

Correct: Make a summary of the meeting and send a copy to all departments; then, have managers forward their comments.

(Join the first two clauses with *and*; add the third after a semicolon.)

Run-on: The photocopiers now in use are <u>faulty they</u> keep breaking <u>down and</u> it is costly and an <u>inconvenience with</u> a backlog of documents to be copied.

Correct: The photocopiers now in use are faulty and keep breaking down. With a backlog of documents to be copied, this problem is inconvenient and costly.

(Create two sentences.)

> **NOTE:** Fused and run-on sentences are serious writing errors. A fused sentence lacks the punctuation needed to arrange ideas. A run-on sentence squeezes too many ideas into one sentence. Both of these errors make a sentence confusing.

PARALLEL STRUCTURE

A sentence is **parallel** when similar elements in the sentence are constructed the same way. The reader can anticipate the meaning of the sentence because the similar elements are logically presented.

HINT: create parallels by repeating prepositions (*in, at, from*, etc.), articles (*a, an, the*), and the word *to* in the infinitive form.

He worked in Asia, in China, and in Thailand.

Representatives came from England, from Ireland, and from France.

Her job was to find clients and to monitor their accounts.

Faulty parallelism occurs when sentence elements have equal function but dissimilar form.

Examples: (the faulty parallel element is underlined)

Faulty Parallel: The director took responsibility for hiring, firing, and recruits.

Correct Parallel: The director took responsibility for hiring, firing, and recruiting. (gerund form is consistent)

Faulty Parallel: The company paid for professional development courses in computer graphics, elements of design, and technician trainees.

Correct Parallel: The company paid for professional development courses in computer graphics, in elements of design, and in technician training. (noun form repeated)

Faulty Parallel: She learned to write effective business letters and contacting clients.

Correct Parallel: She learned to write effective business letters and to contact clients. (infinite form repeated)

NOTE: For the sake of balance and clarity, it is often useful to write out the infinite form in full for each part of the parallel statement.

Example: She learned to write business letters, create presentations, and deal with customers. *Becomes...*
She learned **to** write business letters, **to** create presentations, and **to** deal with customers.
(The repeated infinite form is more formal and balanced.)

> "The most valuable of all talents is that of never using two words when one will do."
> *Thomas Jefferson*

WORDINESS

Wordiness occurs with the use of unnecessary words and phrases including redundant expressions. The business writer should keep composition concise and direct by using precise vocabulary. Some writers feel that a wordy expression gives an air of sophistication: nothing could be further from the truth.

Here are examples of wordiness with alternative constructions.

1) What a manager should do when writing out instructions is to be careful that the instructions are precise and clear.

improved

A manager should write clear, precise instructions.

Avoid the overuse of "there are" or "it is":

2) The reason that there are so many reports is that there are so many possible markets to consider.

improved

Many reports are needed because of so many markets to consider.

3) Is it a known fact that hard work will lead to a promotion.

improved

Hard work will lead to a promotion.

Avoid repetition:

4) Once the business was set up, the work of building a profitable business began.

improved

Once the business was set up, the work of making it profitable began.

5) The group made the final decision and stood by that decision.

improved

The group stood by their final decision.

NOTE: In example (5), the repetition of the word "decision" may be effective for emphasis.

> "The finest language is mostly made up of simple unimposing words."
> *George Eliot*

REDUNDANCY

Another term for redundancy is tautology: a form of repeating an idea rather than just a single word. If, for example, you begin a sentence with "In my opinion, I think..." you are being redundant. You cannot "think" in any opinion but your own. Also, a statement such as "He dealt with issues in succession, one after the other" is clearly repetitive.

Frequently used redundant expressions

basic fundamentals	future projections
but nevertheless	large in size
close scrutiny	more preferable
continue on	necessary prerequisite
very unique	new innovation
desirable benefits	other alternatives
end results	past history
enter into	revert back

WORDY PHRASES

A writer should replace a wordy, tired phrase with a single word. Jargon and buzzwords should also be avoided.

at that point in time	then
at the present time	now
be of the opinion that	think
because of the fact that	because
by means of	by
due to the fact that	because
during the time that	while
in the event that	if
make reference	refer
on many occasions	often
the fact that	because

MISPLACED AND DANGLING MODIFIERS

Modifiers such as adjectives, adverbs, and certain phrases and clauses enhance writing. These should be used for description and clarification purposes and should be placed close to the terms they modify.

Examples: (problem areas are underlined)

Weak: Tentatively she was in charge of her department.
(This means she was tentative.)
Better: She was tentatively in charge of her department.
(This means her being in charge was tentative.)

Weak: He works to catch up on weekends.
Better: He works on weekends to catch up.

Weak: They purchased laptops from a small outlet that cost $450.00.
Better: They purchased laptops that cost $450.00 from a small outlet.

Weak: The client nearly requested a whole new marketing strategy.
Better: The client requested nearly a whole new marketing strategy.

Weak: The manager spoke of necessary changes in the meeting.
Better: In the meeting, the manager spoke of necessary changes.

Weak: The files are in the cabinet that we use to complete the report.
Better: The files we use to complete the report are in the cabinet.

MISUSED MODIFIERS

1) Customer Service handled complaints ~~quick~~ quickly.

2) His boss thought that his work was completed ~~real~~ really well.

3) Once the report was complete, everything seemed ~~differently~~ different from previously thought.

COMPARISONS

1) Paul is **more** dedicated than Eric, and the **most** dedicated of the employees.

(Use *more* for comparison of two; *most* for comparison of more than two.)

2) The private investor was **more** informed than his advisor.

3) He knows the market **better than** Phillip. (than Phillip does)

4) Of the three salespersons, Susan is **the most** successful.

COMMA USE

Next to the full stop (a period), the comma is perhaps the most used punctuation; unfortunately, it is also the most misused. Too often commas are sprinkled throughout a document without regard for the rules of comma use. Primarily, the comma helps clarify and give order to a statement. It is also a handy tool for creatively expressing ideas by strategically arranging sentence elements.

Use a comma to separate words and phrases in a series.

Examples:

1) The office administrator bought the following items: computers, scanners, and stationery. (See Oxford comma, p. 30.)

2) A good sales plan includes solid research, creative marketing, and the setting of realistic goals.

3) The board members reached an agreement by having an open discussion, by examining the documents, and by holding a vote.

NOTE: Some newspaper style guides eliminate the comma (referred to as the Oxford comma) before the "and" that introduces the final item in a list. For the sake of clarity, this comma should always be included. (See Oxford comma, p. 30.)

Use a comma between adjectives preceding a noun.

Examples:

1) The office tower was a modern, architecturally splendid building.

2) He gave an inspiring, informative presentation.

NOTE: With concurrent adjectives, test for correct comma use by replacing the comma with the word "and" between adjectives; if "and" fits, then the original comma placement was correct: *It was a bright, sunny day* or *it was a bright and sunny day*.

Use a comma to set off words in apposition.

A word or phrase in apposition has the same meaning as the term to which it refers.

Examples: (the apposition is underlined)

1) The chairperson, <u>Susan Weston</u>, convened the meeting.

2) The issues, <u>funding and staffing</u>, will be priorities.

Use a comma to set off a contrasting idea.

Examples:

1) Business writing should be clear, not confusing.

2) The better route to a solution is analysis, not guesswork.

3) The effective manager has precise goals, but keeps an open mind.

Use a comma to set off a transition.

Examples:

1) On the contrary, the board meeting was of vital importance.

2) Nevertheless, new computers would increase productivity.

3) As a matter of course, he decided to go with the original plan.

Use a comma to set off a dependent clause or a prepositional phrase that begins a sentence.

Examples:

1) Although the market is down today, the future looks bright.

2) In fact, the opposite reaction occurred when the market fell.

Use a comma to separate the two parts of a compound sentence when the second part of the sentence expands the main idea or when clarity is needed.

Examples:

1) For years the company had been planning to expand globally, and the executive committee has now decided to go ahead.

2) There were three companies bidding on the contract, but it was decided that these applicants were unsuitable.

3) The company president initiated new incentives, and the staff responded with increased proficiency in all areas.

> **NOTE:** If the introductory clause or phrase is short, no comma is necessary.
>
> 1) When every one arrived the meeting began.
>
> 2) The decision having been made the proposal went forward.

Use a comma with dates.

Examples:

1) July 22, 2012

2) August, 2012

3) May 2013 (It is also acceptable to leave out the comma.)

Use a comma with numbers or similar words in succession.

Examples:

1) On January 15, 35 employees were laid off.

2) We must accept that what is, is right.

The terms *yes*, *why*, *well*, or *no* beginning a sentence should be set off by a comma.

Examples:

1) Well, we have reconsidered the offer and we must refuse.

2) No, there has been no change in our plans.

3) Yes, we anticipate that her appointment will be announced.

If *well* or *why* appears within a sentence, a comma is not needed.

Examples:

1) He presented his case very well.

2) They questioned why we would move forward with the proposal.

Do not place a comma in front of a verb unless it is the second comma of a parenthetic term or a term in apposition.

Incorrect: The manager and her staff, attended the meeting.

Correct: The manager and her staff attended the meeting.

Correct: The manager and her staff, who were all presenters, attended the meeting.

A case for the "Oxford comma" (the final comma in a series)

1) He presented the case to his partners, Juan and Sophia.

Sentence (1) suggests that the partners are made up of Juan and Sophia and that <u>possibly</u> the "case" was presented to only those two.

2) He presented the case to his partners, Juan, and Sophia.

Sentence (2) means that the case was presented to the partners and to two other persons—Juan and Sophia.

COLON, SEMICOLON, DASH

The colon, semicolon, and dash are used to arrange information logically, to clarify the main idea of a sentence, or to add emphasis.

THE COLON

Use a colon to introduce a list.

Example:

> The Purchasing Agent ordered the following items in bulk: photocopy paper, printer cartridges, file folders, and pens.

Example: (with a numbered list)

> According to the seminar presenter, the three factors for success are as follows:
> 1) Continuing Education
> 2) Mentorship
> 3) Professional Development

Do not use a colon after a verb.

Example:

Incorrect: The seminar presenter used: graphs, charts, and samples.

Correct: The seminar presenter used graphs, charts, and samples.

Do not use a colon if the list is closely connected to the verb.

Example:

> The factory workers requested better safety equipment, improved lighting, and overhead fans. (no colon after *requested*)

Use a colon to introduce a quotation or formal statement.

Examples:

> 1) The consultant stated: "80% of success is planning."
>
> 2) One of the principles of the corporation was written as follows: Every employee has the right to be treated with respect.

NOTE: If a complete sentence that follows a colon stands apart, it begins with a capital letter.

Use a colon to highlight an appositive that further explains a statement or restates an idea.

Examples:

1) There is only one thing that matters to the CFO: making money.

2) Making money is the only thing that matters to the CFO.
   (Above is the same statement as sentence (1) but without emphasis.)

3) The college has one goal: the success of all students.

4) The success of all students is the one goal of the college.
   (Above is the same statement as sentence (3), but less emphatic.)

THE COLON: (other uses)

Use a colon with time and ratios.

time 2:30 p.m.   **ratio** 4 to 1 becomes 4:1

Use a colon with a salutation.

Dear Ms. Smith: or   Ladies and Gentlemen:

Use a colon after the abbreviation *for example* (i.e.).

Most mornings we begin work at 9:00 a.m., but sometimes it varies, i.e.: on Tuesdays we have a staff meeting at 7:00 a.m.

THE SEMICOLON

Use a semicolon to join independent clauses (sentences); a semicolon precedes transitional terms such as *however, nevertheless, although, but*, and *for example*.

Examples:

1) The figures indicated a banner year; next year could be better.
   (Above are two short sentences with a common topic.)

2) The managers worked hard; thus, their bonuses were generous.
   (*Thus* is a transitional term that follows the semicolon.)

3) The company has offered to pay for training courses for employees; however, failure to succeed in a course will result in withdrawal of financial support; this, it is felt, is a fair condition of the funding.
   (Above, two semicolons join <u>three</u> related independent clauses.)

Use a semicolon to separate items in a series when there is internal punctuation, when names have titles or addresses, and when coordinating clauses are long or contain commas.

Examples:

(internal punctuation in phrases in a series)

1) The MBA course covers areas of study such as: the need for in-house professional development; new business development, including overseas expansion; formal communication—for business purposes—in the workplace and beyond.

(names with titles)

2) The speakers at the seminar were R.L. Singh, Business Communications; David Wise, CEO, Greenlink Consulting; Ana Zahili, Director of Personnel, Stitko Precision Systems.

(names with addresses)

3) Invitations to the company dinner will be sent to the following: Mr. Richard Desousa, 221 Balsam Road; Paulo Rinaldi, 43 Nicholas Street; Susan Wong, 216 Carriage Road.

(separating coordinating clauses)

4) An excellent business writer does not use jargon or slang; follows format guidelines; ensures that the message is clear.

Use a semicolon instead of a colon when introducing a list that begins with the following terms: *namely, for instance, as for example.*

Examples:

1) The presentation will address actual sales situations; **namely,** market research, client solicitation, high-tech presentations, and the consultative approach.

2) There will be a new meeting schedule posted soon; **for instance,** our regular Monday morning meeting will be moved to Tuesday afternoon and the Wednesday end-of-day meeting will be moved to Friday morning.

3) Summer work hours are being reviewed for next year; **for example,** many employees would like extended daily hours leading to a four-day work week.

THE DASH

A dash is less formal than a colon and is used primarily for the emphasis or the clarification of a preceding statement in a sentence. A dash is also used to indicate an abrupt interruption in a sentence or to express a spread in time (1960–1980). Like a colon, a dash may introduce a finishing statement that clarifies a previous point made in a sentence. Colons, on the other hand, tend to be stronger finishers that introduce a conclusive idea. In business writing, dashes should be used sparingly.

There are two kinds of dashes:

1) the *en* dash, roughly the width of the letter **n** (–)
2) the *em* dash, roughly the width of the letter **m** (—)

Use the *n* dash to join words showing distance.

Example:

the London–Paris express train

Use the *m* dash to set off a word, a phrase, or a clause.

Example:

Canada—land mass nine million sq. km—is second to Russia in size.

Use the *m* dash after a series when the main clause follows the list.
(The reverse of this structure would have the main clause appear first and introduce the list with a colon.)

Example:

South Korea, Thailand, and Viet Nam—these are countries poised for economic growth.

Use a dash to highlight a parenthetical section in a sentence.

Commas are often used to set off a parenthetical construction; but a dash is more emphatic and highlights the parallel.

Example:

The late stock market rally—much to the delight of investors—indicated substantial gains.

NOTE: The *en* and *em* dashes (–,—) are usually found under "special characters" in a word processing program. Microsoft and Apple operating systems have short keys for both types of dashes.

Use a dash when a parenthetical segment includes commas.

Example:

> Our international business locations—Singapore, Hong Kong, and Shanghai—are expanding at an exponential rate.

Use a dash before an end word or phrase that adds a degree of emphasis or explanation to the main idea.

Examples:

> 1) There was one final consideration—how to invest the profits.
>
> 2) He has only one person to blame—himself.

PARENTHESES, BRACKETS, QUOTATIONS, ELLIPSES

PARENTHESES

A parenthetical element is additional information not necessary to the main idea of a sentence, but too important to leave out.

Use parentheses to indicate additional information.

Examples:

> 1) The report (bound in hardcover) was given to each manager.
> 2) The corporation applied for an extension of credit (soon to be approved), which will fund the building of a new plant.

Parentheses may be used with letters or numbers in a list.

Examples:

The agenda was as follows:
  (a) Introductory Remarks
  (b) Guest Speaker
  (c) Productivity Workshop

He planned the following steps:
  (1) contact potential new clients
  (2) hold an information session
  (3) arrange follow-up meetings

NOTE: If the parenthetic element is a complete sentence, the period goes inside the closing parenthesis:
Australia has a population of 21.5 million. (It ranks 54th in the world.)

BRACKETS [ ]

Add brackets within a quotation to give an explanation or a comment not written by the author of the original text. Also, use [sic] following an error (such as a spelling error) in a quotation.

Examples:

1) adding explanatory information not included in the original text

The mayor stated: "This great city [New York] is the business capital of the world."

2) indicating a spelling error in original text

The text stated: "The population of Malasia [sic] is close to 29 million."(*Malasia* should be spelled *Malaysia)*

3) inside parentheses, use brackets only

Hong Kong is designated as a Special Administrative Region (SAR) and has a free market economy (highly dependent on foreign trade [see appendix A]).

QUOTATION MARKS " "

Quotation marks are seldom needed in business writing; however, they are required in the following cases:

1) to indicate a direct quotation that encloses the exact words of an outside speaker or writer
2) to indicate a quoted word or to highlight a technical term or unusual terminology
3) to indicate a title of a report, a chapter within a book, an essay, a periodical, or an article (book titles are written in italics)

Examples:

1) The guest speaker stated: "Fiscal prudence is the key to the progress of an emerging economy."
2) The uses of "accept" and "except" are often confused.
3) The speaker referred to the article "Modern Economics" to support his main idea.
4) English is now the "de facto" language of business.

ELLIPSES: Use ellipses plus end punctuation to end a sentence.

Ellipses (...) indicate that words have been left out of a quotation: "...yet the market responded positively....But, investors are wary."

MORE ON QUOTATION MARKS

In business writing, it is best to introduce a direct quotation with a colon. However, for a more personal touch, use the appropriate form of the verb *to say* (he *says*, she *said*). Avoid flamboyant or dramatic verbs such as *proclaimed, uttered, exclaimed*, etc.

Examples:

1) The director stated: "Productivity will increase with technology."

2) Her business partner said, "Synergy is our strength."

PUNCTUATION WITH QUOTATION MARKS

1) Place periods and commas inside the closing quotation mark.

2) Place semicolons and colons outside the closing quotation mark.

3) Place question and exclamation marks inside the quotation if they are connected to the quoted material; if not, place them outside.

Examples: (check the placement of punctuation with quotation marks)

1) "Process the client's request immediately," said the supervisor.

2) He submitted his so-called "business expenses"; management was not happy with the numbers.

3) She requested a list of his "business expenses": hotels, travel, and food allowances.

4) "We exceeded sales projections!" the Sales Manager announced.

5) The company wants sales figures to rise "twenty-five percent"!

6) "Where are the spreadsheets?" she asked.

A QUOTATION WITHIN A QUOTATION

A quotation within a quotation is enclosed with single quotation marks.

Examples:

She stated: "The article we should all read is titled 'The Rising Asian Economy'."

LONG QUOTATIONS

Long quotations should be preceded by a colon, indented, and single spaced. Long quotations set off from the body text do not require quotations marks.

> **NOTE:** A quotation can be blended into a sentence if it fits grammatically: The company was, according to Forbes Magazine, the leader in it's field.

THE APOSTROPHE (1)

POSSESSIVE FORM (shows ownership)

SINGULAR NOUNS

To form the possessive of a singular noun, add 's.

administrator's report   chairperson's decision

To form the possessive of a singular noun ending in s, add 's.

Dickens's novels   Forbes's articles

PLURAL NOUNS

To form the possessive of a plural noun ending in s, add '.

accountants' records   employees' concerns

To form the possessive of a plural noun not ending in s, add 's.

women's club   people's choice

To form the possessive of a compound noun, add 's to the last word.

Bank of China's funds   person-of-record's statement

To form the possessive of noun pairs, add 's to the last noun.

Standard & Poor's rating   Klein and Foster's law firm

To form the possessive of nouns of time or money, add 's or '.

previous year's taxes   several days' pay

To form the possessive of individual words in a series add 's to each.

Toyota's, Honda's, and Subaru's new car lineup

NOTE: Use an "of-phrase" in place of an apostrophe to avoid ambiguity, for ease of expression, and with inanimate objects.

(1) the chairperson's dismissal   the dismissal of the chairperson
(2) the business's goals   the goals of the business
(3) the office's window   the window of the office

In example (1) the *of-phrase* avoids the ambiguity over whether the chairperson is being dismissed or is doing the dismissing.
In example (2) the *of-phrase* makes the sentence easier to express.
In example (3) the *of-phrase* is used with an inanimate object.

THE APOSTROPHE (2)

NUMBERS AND ACRONYMS

There are two schools of thought regarding the apostrophe with dates and acronyms. Some writers prefer to use the apostrophe to denote the plural, which can cause confusion over whether the possessive or the plural is intended. Except for lower case letters, it is best to use *s* instead of *'s* when forming the plural.

* To show a time span use an *en dash* between dates (1970s–1990s).

Example:

> 1960s is plural   1960's is possessive

(1960's, although incorrect, is sometimes accepted as a plural; however, it could be mistaken for the possessive form and should be avoided.)

> The **1980s** were a time of technological advancement. (plural)
>
> The **1930's** were a difficult time economically. ('s used for plural)
>
> They enjoyed **'60's** music. (possessive and short form of 1960)
>
> He drove an **'97** BMW. (adjective, short form of 1997)

Example:

> **ABCs** (preferred) or **ABC's** ('s often used, but not preferred)
>
> **a's** and **o's**, **p's** and **q's** (use **'s** for plurals of lowercase letters)

PERSONIFICATION

Use *'s* with inanimate objects that are personified.

> The Stock Exchange's revenge was swift.

CONTRACTIONS

Contractions are formed by combining words and substituting an apostrophe for the letters removed.

cannot – can't	let us – let's	will not – won't
does not – doesn't	was not – wasn't	would not – wouldn't
it is – it's	who is – who's	you will – you'll

Contractions are common in informal writing and in conversation. In business writing, contractions are best used sparingly.

CAPITAL LETTERS

Use capitals for the following:

1) the beginning of a sentence:

The meeting was held at corporate headquarters.

2) the beginning of a direct quotation:

Buffett wrote: "Price is what you pay. Value is what you get."

3) a person's name:

Hillary Clinton   William Shakespeare   E.P. Taylor

4) official titles and titles before a name:

President Barack Obama	Vice President Joe Biden
Prime Minister Singh	(the) Earl of Sussex
Sir Edmund Hillary	Albert II, Prince of Monaco
Cardinal Vidal	Chief Justice John Roberts
Mother Teresa	Mayor Bloomberg

> **NOTE:** When the designation is not used to specify a person but is used as a general term, no capital is required.

She hoped to become prime minister one day.
It is the responsibility of a president to make decisions.
The cardinals and bishops gathered in Rome.

5) abbreviations and professional designations following a name:

Martin Luther King, Jr.   Lee Jones, Barrister and Solicitor
Brian May, Ph.D.   Clarence Darrow, Attorney at Law

6) titles of relatives before a name or in place of a name:

Aunt Sana   Cousin Tariq   Uncle Paul

> **NOTE:** When the term for a relative replaces the relative's name, the term acts as a proper noun.

We will have dinner with Grandfather, and Mother will join us.

7) days of the week, months, and holidays:

April   Monday   New Year's Eve   Ramadan   Christmas

8) academic courses or subjects:

Business 301   Studies in Greek Mythology   World History

> **NOTE:** When an educational course name is nonspecific, no capital is needed.
> She studied geography. He enjoyed science, but preferred history.

CAPITAL LETTERS

9) a proper name used as an adjective:

Shakespearean sonnet   Dickensian Christmas

10) religious documents and names:

Allah   the Lord   Buddhism   the Bible   Judaism

11) geographical names and regions:

Amazon River	London, England
Antarctica	New York City
Asia	North America
Bay of Bengal	Pacific Ocean
Cape of Good Hope	South China Sea
Ho Chi Minh City	South Korea
Lake Como	Suez Canal

12) other proper names (structures, institutions, events, brands):

Adidas	New York Yankees
Apple	Oxford University
Brooklyn Bridge	Panama Canal
Eiffel Tower	Queen Mary
Great Depression	Tower of London
Great Wall of China	United Auto Workers
Manchester United	World War II

13) literary works, films, plays, songs, etc.:

Use capital letters for first and last words and important words in between.

How to Win Friends and Influence People (book)
Extreme Money: Masters of the Universe and the Cult of Risk (book)
"Wall Street: Money Never Sleeps" (film)
"How to Build a Successful Corporation" (article)

NOTE: Book titles are usually written in italics; titles of poems, songs, plays, films, television shows, and magazine articles are enclosed in quotation marks.

NUMBERS

The basic rules for numbers are as follows:

1) Write out numbers nine and lower.

2) For numbers greater than nine, use numerals.

3) Spell out a number that begins a sentence.

However, when writing out numbers, there are many exceptions and special cases as listed below.

If a sentence begins with a number, spell it out:

Twenty degrees Celsius is equal to 68°F.

To avoid an awkward sentence construction, rewrite a sentence so that it doesn't start with a large number:

In 2010, the per capita GDP of the United Kingdom was £34,800.

> **NOTE:** For large sums, add the words *million* or *billion.*

Use numbers for large quantities, units of measure, page numbers, degrees, and amounts of money:

The population of Singapore (as of July 2011) was 4,740,737.

The coastline of China is 14,500 km (9,000 miles) long.

One US gallon is equal to 3.78 L.

The committee examined page 23 of the report.

The population of Japan is over 126 million.

The 2010 GDP of Japan was $4.31 trillion (US).

Numbers used for identification should be written in numerals:

Air Asia Flight 235 was delayed.

His licence plate number was 333333.

Use numbers for times and dates:

Hong Kong became a Special Administration Region (SAR) on July 1, 1997.

The meeting began at 8:15 a.m. and lasted until 6:30 p.m.

Flight 445 departed at 13:10 and arrived at 18:25.

Spell out number adjectives that can be written as one or two words:

Barack Obama is the forty-fourth president of the United States.

In 2014, it will be one hundred years since the start of WW1.

NUMBERS

Use numbers for addresses (spell out numbered street names):

The British Prime Minister lives at 10 Downing Street, London.
Tiffany's New York is on Fifth Avenue.

Use numbers for percentages and decimals, except when a percentage begins a sentence:

Ten per cent is considered a healthy return on investment.
The literacy rate in South Korea is 97.9 per cent. (avoid "%")

Use words for fractions; hyphenate fractions used as adjectives:

China and India combined account for over one third of the
world's population. (noun)
One quarter of the Canadian population is French in origin. (noun)
The reserve fund is one-third full. (adjective)

Use figures for definite ages:

As of April 1 2012, Apple Inc. became a 36-year-old company.
Steve Jobs passed away at 56 years of age.

Use words for indefinite ages:

Tiger Woods was in his twenties when he was ranked number one.

Use figures for results of a vote:

The ballot tally indicated 23 for, 45 against.

In other than technical writing, state dimensions in figures and words:

The monitor screen was 24 in. (61 cm) by 40 in. (102 cm).

All distances should be written in figures and words:

The coastline of Spain is 4,964 kilometres in length.
The coastline of the United States is 11,945 miles in length.

Temperature should be expressed in figures:

The average temperature in Indonesia is 28°C.
The average temperature in New York City in July is 85°F.

Express measures in figures, except fractional measurement:

The volume of Lake Superior is 12,100 cubic km.
At one point, the depth of the Grand Canyon is 6,000 feet.
The car needed one-half litre of oil.

SPELLING RULES

Spelling rules in the English language are problematic because there are many exceptions. However, it is useful to know the basic rules of spelling and to be aware of notable exceptions.

Rule 1: Place *i* before *e* except after *c* or when the *ei* gives an *ay* sound such as in the word weigh.

achieve, believe, chief, friend, field, piece, relieve, yield ceiling, conceive, receive, receipt, perceive, weigh

Exceptions:

counterfeit, foreign, forfeit, height, leisure, neither, seize, weird

Rule 2: Drop the silent *e* at the end of a word before a suffix that begins with a vowel.

arrive + al = arrival	guide + ance = guidance
exercise + ing = exercising	desire + able = desirable
continue + ance = continuance	future + istic = futuristic

Exceptions:

To avoid spelling confusion or to maintain a soft sounding *ce* or *ge*, add *ing*, *ous*, or *able* to words ending in *e*:

be + ing = being (not bing)	notice + able = noticeable
dye + ing = dyeing (not dying)	peace + able = peaceable
courage + ous = courageous	salvage + able = salvageable

Rule 3: If the suffix begins with a consonant, keep the silent *e*.

encourage + ment = encouragement
extreme + ly = extremely
nine + ty = ninety
force + ful = forceful

Exceptions:

acknowledge + ment = acknowledgment / acknowledgement
(US)   (UK/CA)

argue + ment = argument

judge + ment = judgment / judgement
(US)   (UK/CA)

true + ly = truly   whole + ly = wholly   nine + th = ninth

Rule 4: Change *y* to *i* for words with a *y* after a consonant.

busy + er = busier   rely + able = reliable

Exceptions:

carry = carrying   hurry = hurrying   study = studying

Rule 5: If a word ends in *y* following a vowel, keep the *y* and add the suffix.

buy + ing = buying   obey + ing = obeying

Rule 6: With words ending in *c*, the *c* sound can be soft *se* or hard *ke*. If the *c* sound is soft, just add the prefix; if the *c* sound is hard, before adding *e*, *i*, or *y*, add *k*. Also, when adding *a*, *o*, or *u*, the *c* sound is unchanged.

criticism (turns to soft *c*)   critical (hard *c*)   panicky (hard *c*)

Rule 7: For words ending in *s* or an *es* sound (*ss*, *x*, *sh*), form the plural by adding *es*.

bus = busses   class = classes   dish = dishes   fox = foxes

Rule 8: final consonants

  For words ending in *ic* add *ally*.

basic = basically   characteristic = characteristically

  For adjectives ending in *l* add *ly*.

casual = casually   exceptional = exceptionally
final = finally   usual = usually

  For words ending in *n*, keep the *n* and add *ness*.

meanness   plainness

  For words ending with two consonants, just add the suffix.

help = helped   confirm = confirmation

  For words with a final consonant preceded by two vowels, do not double the final consonant.

cheat = cheated   meet = meeting   retail = retailing

NOTE: Unlike British and Canadian usage, American usage does not double final the consonant before a vowel with a short sound.
benefiting (US) / benefitting (UK/CA) canceled (US) / cancelled (UK/CA)
marvelous (US) / marvellous (UK/CA) traveled (US) / travelled (UK/CA)

FREQUENTLY MISSPELLED WORDS

NOTE: words that appear in the "Commonly Confused Words" section (pages 150–157) are not listed below.

A
abbreviate
abhorrent
absence
accessible
accommodate
acknowledge
advantageous
agreeable
analysis
ancillary
anonymous
apparatus
argument
ascertain
authority
auxiliary

B
bankruptcy
beneficial
bookkeeper
brochure
bulletin

C
calendar
campaign
category
ceiling
circuit
coercion
coexist
coherent
column
commission

commitment
committee
competent
competitor
comptroller
conceivable
concise
congratulations
conscientious
consensus
continuous
cooperation
copyright
copywriter
correspondence

D
debtor
deceit
deferred
descent
dilemma
disappearance
disastrous
discipline
dissatisfied

E
efficient
eighth
eligible
embarrassment
enforceable
environment
exaggerated
excel

excessive
exhibitor
existence
exorbitant
exploitative
extraordinary

F
facility
facsimile
familiar
fascinating
feasible
fiery
financeable
foreign
forewarn
forfeit
foreseeable
fourth
fraudulent
freight

G
gauge
government
gracious
grammar
grievance
guarantee

H
harassment
height
heinous
hierarchy
hindrance

FREQUENTLY MISSPELLED WORDS

I
immediately
impeccable
incisive
independent
inferred
innocence

J
jealous
judicious

K
knowledgeable

L
legitimate
leisure
litigious

M
maintenance
malicious
mandatory
mathematics
mediator
millennium
miscellaneous
misspell
misstatement
mitigate
mortgage
myriad

N
necessary
negligible
negotiate
neutral
ninety
noticeable

O
obsolescent
occasionally
occurrence
omission
omitted
outrageous
overrated

P
pacify
pamphlet
panacea
parallel
perceive
personnel
phenomenon
piece
plausible
possession
precise
preferred
prejudice
prerequisite
professional

Q
questionnaire
quiet
quite
quorum

R
receipt
receive
recommend
reconciliation
recurrence
reenactment

reference
referred
remembrance
remittance
renown

S
scarcely
schedule
scheme
seizure
separate
serviceable

T
tariff
tendency
thorough
transferring
transmittal
truly

U
unconscious
undoubtedly
unmistakable
upheaval

V
vacuum
vehemently
vendor
versatile
vicious
vulnerable

W
warranty
wholly

Z
zealous

COMPOUND WORDS AND HYPHENATION

The ongoing evolution of compound words is sometimes a result of the frequency of use or the universal acceptance of the joining of two words. For example, two words in sequence may form a single idea and after constant use, end up hyphenated. From that point these words may evolve to form a single word. Therefore, it is difficult to attach fixed rules to when or when not to hyphenate words or to combine them as one.

There are three types of compound nouns:

1) a term of two separate words:

common sense   risk management

direct marketing   venture capital

2) a term of two words hyphenated:

year-end   high-tech

co-op   all-inclusive

3) a term of two words combined:

benchmark   shareholder

boardroom   trademark

NOTE: When in doubt, refer to a dictionary. For certain compound words, a British dictionary frequently prefers the two-word spelling while an American dictionary may prefer the one-word compound.

Clarity in meaning governs the form of a compound word.
Here are examples of how combining words avoids confusion.

1) Global warming is an example of the **greenhouse** effect.

2) They bought the **green house** on the corner.

3) The farmers belong to a **co-op**.

4) The chickens were kept in a chicken **coop**.

NOTE: 1) a **hyphen** (-) joins words creating compound words

2) an **en** dash (–) shows space between two things (locations) or a span of time (Honk Kong–Shanghai) (2010–2012)

3) an **em** dash (—) sets off words and phrases in a sentence, allows for an emphatic ending, or creates a parenthetic construction.

Rules of Forming Compound Words

Use hyphens to combine two words used as an adjective; but do not hyphenate words used as adjectives when one of them is an adverb (ending in *ly*) or a comparative term:

1) He referred to an **up-to-date** case study.

2) She was a **well-respected** business analyst.

3) The executive always booked a **first-class** flight.

4) He executed a **perfectly planned** strategy. (no hyphen with *ly*)

5) She was the **most** quoted business consultant. (comparative)

6) On his corporate **credit card** he had a large **credit-card** debt.

> **Note:** in the above examples, the compounds used as adjectives are hyphenated.

Use a hyphen for generally accepted word combinations:

fact-finder, father-in-law, not for profit, x-ray, fund-raising

Do not use a hyphen for chemical terms:

hydrogen peroxide solution

Do not use a hyphen for terms mixed with numbers or letters:

Type II Diabetes

Use a hyphen for words beginning with *all, ex, inter, self*.

all-inclusive, ex-president, self-improvement

Use a hyphen to clarify meaning:

re-sign *versus* resign; re-creation *versus* recreation
resign means to quit; re-sign means to sign again
re-creation meant to create again; recreation refers to a leisure activity

Do not use a hyphen with the following prefixes:

anti, bi, co, counter, de, dis, hyper, in, inter, mega, micro, mis, non,
out, over, post, pre, re, semi, un, under.

COMPOUND BUSINESS TERMS

A
account executive
add-on
after market
annual report
antitrust

B
base pay
benchmark
biannual
brainstorming
branch office
byproduct

C
cash flow
cooperative
cosign
counterclaim
cross-check
cutbacks

D
database
deadline
de facto
direct marketing
downgrade

E
entry-level
ex officio

F
face value
fair trade
first class
flex time
forecast
foreman
front office

G
go-between
groundwork
guidebook

H
hard copy
head hunter
headquarters
human resources

I
input
internship

J
joint venture
journeyman
junk bond

K
keynote
keyword

L
laissez-faire
layoff
leasehold
leave of absence

M
markdown
market share
mass media
middleman
multimedia

O
off-line
offset
outsourcing
overhead

P
payout
petty cash
prepaid
pro bono
pro forma
public offering

Q
quid pro quo

R
risk management

S
semiannual
shareholder
stock option

T
test market
trademark
turnkey

U
undervalued
upkeep

V
venture capital

W
warehouse
workforce

Y
year-end

> "England and America are two countries divided by a common language."   *George Bernard Shaw*

The British, American, and Canadian spellings of numerous terms differ. Canadian spelling generally follows British rules especially with the "our" instead of the "or" ending; however, with the "ize" and the "ise" endings, Canadian spelling follows American spelling using the "ize" ending.

(Terms that <u>always</u> take the "ise" ending are listed on the next page.)

BRITISH	AMERICAN	CANADIAN
acknowledgement	acknowledgment	acknowledgement
aeroplane	airplane	airplane
aluminium	aluminum	aluminum
amortisation	amortization	amortization
analyse	analyze	analyze
apologise	apologize	apologize
authorise	authorize	authorize
behaviour	behavior	behaviour
calibre	caliber	calibre
cancellation	cancelation	cancellation
candour	candor	candour
capitalise	capitalize	capitalize
catalog	catalogue	catalogue
categorise	categorize	categorize
centimetre	centimeter	centimetre
centre	center	centre
characterise	characterize	characterize
cheque	check	cheque
civilisation	civilization	civilization
colour	color	colour
commercialise	commercialize	commercialize
computerise	computerize	computerize
critise	criticize	criticize
customise	customize	customize
defence	defense	defence
dependant	dependent	dependant
dialogue	dialog	dialogue
economise	economize	economize
endeavour	endeavor	endeavour
enrolment	enrollment	enrolment
familiarise	familiarize	familiarize
favourite	favorite	favourite

The list continues on the next page.

BRITISH	AMERICAN	CANADIAN
finalise	finalize	finalize
flavour	flavor	flavour
fulfil	fulfill	fulfil
generalise	generalize	generalize
grey	gray	grey
harbour	harbor	harbour
honour	honor	honour
humour	humor	humour
industrialise	industrialize	industrialize
initialise	initialize	initialize
instalment	installment	instalment
jewellery	jewelry	jewellery
judgment	judgement	judgment
kilometre	kilometer	kilometre
knowledgeable	knowledgeable	knowledgeable
labelled	labeled	labelled
labour	labor	labour
legalise	legalize	legalize
licence	license	licence
likeable	likable	likable
litre	liter	litre
liveable	livable	livable
minimise	minimize	minimize
moveable	movable	movable
manoeuvre	maneuver	manoeuvre
marvellous	marvelous	marvellous
maximise	maximize	maximize
mediaeval	medieval	medieval
metre	meter	metre
neighbour	neighbor	neighbour
neutralise	neutralize	neutralize
organisation	organization	organization
personalise	personalize	personalize
prioritise	prioritize	prioritize
* programme	* program	* programme
realise	realize	realize
recognise	recognize	recognize
re-examine	reexamine	reexamine
saleable	salable	saleable
signalling	signaling	signalling
sceptical	skeptical	skeptical
specialisation	specialization	specialization
totalling	totaling	totalling
unionise	unionize	unionize
utilise	utilize	utilize
visualise	visualize	visualize

Below is a list of words that have the "ize" sound but are always spelled with the "ise" ending.

advertise
advise
apprise
arise
compromise
demise
despise
devise
disguise
excise
franchise
improvise
incise
merchandise
revise
rise
supervise
surmise
televise

* British and Canadian spelling uses "program" when referring to computers.

THE PRINCIPLES OF BUSINESS WRITING

Business writing takes many forms each suited to a specific purpose. All business writing must be clear and concise with simple, straightforward language.

In the business world, poorly written communication is unacceptable. Every letter, memorandum, report, or announcement must be composed for maximum effect and to suit both the purpose and the intended audience.

STEPS TO SUCCESSFUL BUSINESS WRITING

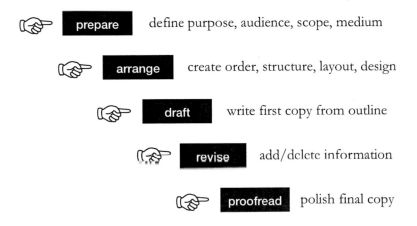

prepare	define purpose, audience, scope, medium
arrange	create order, structure, layout, design
draft	write first copy from outline
revise	add/delete information
proofread	polish final copy

What is the purpose of the communication?

How much detail is needed?

For whom is the communication written?

What is the best format to clearly convey the message?

What action or outcome is expected?

STRUCTURE

To write effectively, it is critical to adhere to a structure. Structure will control the flow of ideas and ensure that what you write is logically presented and readily understood.

Structure = Logical Presentation of Ideas

The Paragraph	made up of sentences dealing with one main idea
Topic Sentence	introduces the main idea of a paragraph
Development Sentences	support and develop the main idea of the paragraph

THE PARAGRAPH

A paragraph is made up of closely related sentences that deal with a common topic or idea sometimes referred to as the **controlling idea**. A paragraph is often a part of a larger body of text.

THE TOPIC SENTENCE

The purpose of a topic sentence is to introduce the main idea of a paragraph. Usually a topic sentence appears at the beginning of a paragraph, but it may appear near the middle or at the end. For example, if in the beginning of a paragraph a question is raised or a notable fact given, the topic sentence may be most effective in the second or third position in the paragraph.

THE DEVELOPMENT SENTENCES

The purpose of the development sentences is to elaborate on the controlling idea introduced in the topic sentence. This can be done by including facts, examples, references, or any information that enhances the reader's understanding of the message. It is important that the development sentences stay on topic.

> **NOTE:** Not all business communication requires paragraph format; however, proper structure is always important to ensure that information is presented clearly and logically.

THE OUTLINE PROCESS

Writing an outline helps you to arrange your ideas, to assess the relevance of your research, and to structure your communication logically.

Once a writer determines the purpose and the audience, it is essential to develop an outline. All business documents should evolve from an outline that defines the scope of the topic, of the sub-topics, and of the sections.

An outline is the end product of brainstorming.

Notes

Go over notes to add or delete information. Create a hierarchy of topics ranging from important to less important and arrange sections or sub-topics accordingly.

Research

List the supplementary information that matches the related topics or sections. Include quotations, statistics, illustrations, and graphs, and any other supportive material.

Order

Establish an order and a guide to the communication using headings and subheadings.

Revise

Review the outline and make changes. If necessary, rearrange the order of sub-topics and sections to allow for a logical flow. Delete redundant headings, subheadings, or sections.

Once the outline is complete, begin your first draft.

THE DRAFT

It is tempting for a writer to try completing a document without an outline and a draft. This is a mistake. The obvious benefit of a draft is that it is **unfinished**, which means you can revise, revise, revise. In short, creating a draft is not an option—it is a necessity. Refer to your outline frequently as you write your draft. Business documents may vary in length and form, but all documents benefit from having originated from a draft.

Start Writing

Write freely and spontaneously. You may begin by making an introductory comment or by stating a particular point or argument. The important thing is to start writing.

Keep Writing

Keep writing. Any uncertainties or problems can be handled later. Make sideline notes as you write for later reference and revision.

Refer to Your Outline

If your writing gets stalled, refer to your outline and your notes to make sure you are including all the important points.

Print and Review

Rearrange paragraphs or sections in strategic order. Look for transitional words that connect ideas. Check that all key points from the outline are covered. Once the initial draft is complete, print it out. Read it aloud to verify the intended tone of the piece.

Create Second Draft

Once a first draft is complete, the document should be thoroughly checked over. Now is the time to revise the vocabulary, to check that sentences are varied in length, and to make sure points are presented logically. Next, begin the second draft.

THE TOPIC SENTENCE

A topic sentence introduces the main idea of a paragraph and may include a brief comment about that idea. A paragraph should consist of only one topic, and should develop that topic through the sentences that follow.

The Topic Sentence = main idea + elaboration

Examples: effective topic sentences

1) The collective effort of all employees was the reason for our company's success this year.

topic sentence = collective effort + company's success

(The developing sentences would elaborate on the *efforts* and the *success*.)

2) To facilitate our global initiatives, three new locations— Singapore, Hong Kong, and Seoul—have been identified for business expansion.

topic sentence = three locations + global initiatives

(The developing sentences would elaborate on *locations* and *initiatives*.)

> **NOTE:** Introduce only the main idea in the topic sentence. Do not include details that will be part of the body of the paragraph.

Example: ineffective topic sentence

3) The three new locations—Singapore, Hong Kong, Seoul—have been targeted for business expansion, and in these locations we intend to set up distribution outlets to serve Southeast Asia.

Example (3) contains too many ideas and gives details that should be reserved for the body of the paragraph. Example topic sentence (2) is much more succinct and functional. It tells just enough to introduce the paragraph.

> **NOTE:** Unify the paragraph by making sure each sentence in the paragraph relates to the main idea. A rephrased (not a repeated) topic sentence may be included at the end of a paragraph for emphasis and to reinforce the main idea.

ORGANIZING IDEAS

A paragraph or a section of a document is **coherent** when its elements blend making it easy for the reader to follow the main idea. Coherency also means consistency in tone and subject.

METHODS OF PRESENTING IDEAS

Chronological Order: In a chronological presentation, information is presented in sequence. Though a technique typically used in narrative writing, chronological order might be used in business writing to clarify a specific order of events or to explain a process: for instance, the sequence of events leading up to a business deal.

Spatial Order: Frequently used in descriptive writing, spatial order, like a camera moving around a room, finds a starting point and then moves around focusing on details or key points as they appear.

Logical Order: This technique is particularly suited to business communication as it arranges information to suit logical associations. It also allows the freedom to present illustrations, explanations, cause-and-effect relationships, and problem-solving action. Two arrangements of presenting ideas lie within this category:

+ general-to-specific (See p. 72–74).
+ specific-to-general

In a **general-to-specific** arrangement, the topic sentence presents a general idea that requires elaboration or explanation. The sentences that follow expand on the topic sentence.

In a **specific-to-general** arrangement the topic sentence states the controlling idea of the paragraph and the supporting information the paragraph will give.

A topic sentence does two things:

1) **introduces** the main (controlling) idea of a paragraph

2) **restricts** the paragraph to a single (controlling) idea

SAMPLE PARAGRAPHS

The paragraphs below are examples of logical and chronological order, and each begins with a clear topic sentence (controlling idea). The body of each paragraph contains sentences that give important details elaborating on the main idea.

(topic sentences in italics)

Logical Order

Three new locations have been identified for business expansion that will facilitate our global initiatives. These locations—Singapore, Hong Kong, and Seoul—have a collective population of over 22 million and represent a significant opportunity for inroads to business in Southeast Asia. The plan is to set up printing operations and distribution outlets in each of these cities. These three new locations are ideal starting points for business expansion as each has a large population and a strategic geographic proximity to other Southeast Asian countries.

topic sentence

ideas arranged in logical order

topic sentence restated

Chronological Order

The collective effort of all employees was the reason for our company's success this year. At the beginning of the year we were seeking ways to increase productivity without incurring unmanageable expense. At a general meeting with all employees, the possibility of adding a weekend shift was discussed and later voted on. After an overwhelming vote of acceptance, it was decided that the weekend shift would be available to anyone wishing to earn overtime pay and that this shift would be scheduled on a rotating basis assigned equally to those interested. By year's end, we found that productivity had increased substantially as a direct result of the work of the employees on the weekend shift.

topic sentence

ideas arranged in chronological order

topic sentence restated

THE BUSINESS LETTER

Each type of business correspondence has a specific design, tone, format, and level of formality suited to the purpose of the message and to the intended audience.

THE BUSINESS LETTER

Business letters are always formal. The format consists of letterhead, date, inside address, salutation, subject line (if necessary), complimentary close, and signature.

Business letters should be clear, concise, and void of slang and jargon. Consisting usually of three or four paragraphs, business letters follow a set design where each paragraph deals with one idea and begins with a topic sentence that introduces that idea.

The sections of a Standard Business Letter (block format)

Company Letterhead

Date

Inside Address

Salutation (Dear...)

Subject Line

Paragraph One states the purpose of the letter.

Paragraph Two outlines specific details and explanations.

Paragraph Three mentions the action requested.

Paragraph Four may include a call to action.

Complimentary Close and Signature

SAMPLE BUSINESS LETTER

Company Letterhead

September 19, 2012

Ms. Sharon Boyd, Vice President
ABC Design Inc.
123 Main Street
Toronto, ON M2W 1G6

Dear Ms. Boyd:

SUBJECT: DESIGN SERVICES

The marketing department of Greenlink Consulting is in the early stages of redesigning our corporate image and is presently in search of the services of a design company. One of our long-time clients, Stitko Precision, recommended your company, ABC Design. I am contacting you to arrange a time to meet and discuss our needs and to learn of the range of your services. *(states company's needs and asks for a meeting)*

We intend to make complete changes to our corporate designs, and we are open to new ideas. The following designs are under review: business cards, letterhead, our company logo, our information brochure, our website, and the signage on the outside of our office building. *(lists design requirements)*

Considering design changes ahead of time may facilitate a more targeted meeting. Next week I will forward a package containing copies of our existing designs along with samples of our brochure and photos of our office building exterior. I hope this will give you a starting point in preparation for our meeting. In the meantime, please visit our website to examine our existing webpage layout and to get a sense of the overall impression we attempt to portray. *(call to action)*

Please contact my assistant, Rita Fernandez, to set up a mutually convenient time to meet. I will be out of the office from September 24 through October 10, but will be available any time after that date. *(states availability for meeting and adds contact information)*

Sincerely,

Joanne Chiu

Joanne Chiu
Vice President, Marketing

The Art of Persuasive Writing

> "Rhetoric...the faculty of discovering the means of persuasion in reference to any subject whatsoever."
> *Aristotle*

In business, persuasive writing is integral to sales letters and proposals, as well as any other correspondence that attempts to convince a reader. Persuasive writing is a specific skill distinguished by the writer's ability to establish and prove a clear premise and to present a series of proofs to support it.

The topic sentence usually appears at the beginning of a persuasive paragraph and must clearly state the main premise. The writer will then, in logical order, present sentences containing the points of proof.

Topic Sentence (1): general premise

Lack of proficiency in written English for business is a widespread problem in today's corporate world.

Topic Sentence (2): specific premise

Many corporations understand the need for excellence in business writing and have taken action to increase the proficiency of their staff in this area.

Topic Sentence (3): general premise

Today, English is the worldwide "de facto" language of business.

Topic Sentence (4): specific premise

With English as the "de facto" language of business worldwide, it is critical that companies ensure that their employees are proficient in business writing.

Although the above topic sentences are related in premise, they differ in content. Each **general** premise would be followed by sentences that support and expand upon the broad idea of the topic. Each **specific** premise is more confined to a narrowed idea.

PLACEMENT OF THE TOPIC SENTENCE

In most cases, the **topic sentence** is the first or second sentence in a paragraph. However, when composing a persuasive letter or report, the placement of the topic sentence depends on the strategy for developing the argument.

If the paragraph begins with a **topic sentence**—a statement of the assertion or proposition—it should then be followed by sentences that expand upon and prove that premise.

Consider the following premise to be argued:

> Because English is now the language of business worldwide, international companies will be intent on initiating in-house training that will increase the business-writing proficiency of their employees.

Topic Sentence (in italics) introducing a paragraph:

English is now the language of business worldwide and companies with nonnative English speaking employees are intent on improving the English writing skills of these staff members. According to the HSBC bank, five times more people are learning English in China than there are people in England: This is a clear indication of the worldwide trend towards English language literacy.

The topic sentence above is followed by a thought-provoking statistic. Proof sentences would follow with facts, quotations, and more evidence.

Topic Sentence (in italics) appearing second in a paragraph:

In a recent advertisement, HSBC bank made this statement: "There are five times more people learning English in China than there are people in England." *Since English is now the language of business worldwide, international companies will focus on improving the English literacy skills of their employees.*

The opening statement above offers a compelling statistic that sets up the topic sentence. Proof sentences would start with the third sentence of the paragraph.

In some cases the topic sentence is the last sentence of the paragraph. This only works when the proof sentences lead to a conclusion that is, in fact, the topic sentence. This approach tends to be dramatic and should be used cautiously.

PERSUASIVE WRITING: the proof paragraph

Once the premise of the persuasive letter has been established, it is time to add the sentences that prove the argument. Before composing these sentences, it is beneficial to make an outline that lists all the key proofs of the argument.

SAMPLE OUTLINES

TOPIC SENTENCE (1): general premise

> Lack of proficiency in Business English writing is a pervasive problem in today's corporate world.

Points of proof:

> 1) statistical proof of inefficiency in Business English writing
>
> 2) reasons for this inefficiency
>
> 3) the effects this lack of proficiency has on business
>
> 4) the need for immediate improvement in business writing
>
> 5) the choice of actions to be taken to increase proficiency

TOPIC SENTENCE (2): specific premise

> Many corporations are aware of the need for excellence in Business English writing and have taken action in this area to increase the proficiency of their staff.

Points of proof:

> 1) English as the worldwide language of business
>
> 2) the benefits of excellence in Business English writing
>
> 3) the universal recognition of the need for excellence in Business English writing and for setting up in-house training
>
> 4) statistics from outside sources in support of in-house training
>
> 5) the choice of actions to be taken to increase proficiency

NOTE: Statistics in addition to quotations from authority figures may be added to the proof paragraph to support the argument.

The next step in developing a solid, persuasive argument is to build sentences from the outline (see above) and arrange them in a logical order:

> 1) chronological (order of events)
>
> 2) general-to-specific order (with a broad topic sentence)
>
> 3) specific-to-general order (with a narrowed topic sentence)

THE POWER OF SUBORDINATION (Refer to types of sentences, p. 22–23.)

Let's suppose that we have a clear statement of argument such as:

> It is important that the corporation makes progress in creating markets in Indonesia.

If this premise is prefaced with a response to an anticipated argument in the form of a subordinate clause, it might add validity to the premise. Placing the main point after the subordinate clause sets off the main premise.

Examples: although, because, therefore, and *once* act as subordinating conjunctions introducing the subordinate clauses; the principal clauses are in italics.

1) <u>Although</u> the corporation has not yet established a corporate base in Indonesia, *it is still important that progress be made in creating markets in this region.* (subordinate clause addresses a concern upfront)

2) *New markets in Southeast Asia are a priority* <u>because</u> this region is one of the world's most populated. (subordinate clause is a qualifier)

3) *Indonesia, a region of 250 million people, has the fourth largest population in the world* <u>therefore</u> it represents an ideal region for market expansion. (subordinate clause is a qualifier)

4) Once a corporate presence has been established in Indonesia, *a full-blown marketing initiative will be implemented.* (comma sets off subordinate clause that appears first)

5) *A full-blown marketing initiative will be implemented* once a corporate presence has been established in Indonesia. (no comma)

Examples (4) and (5) state the same idea; however, sentence (4) highlights the establishment of a corporate presence; sentence (5) highlights the idea of implementing a full-blown marketing initiative.

Which is more effective? The answer lies in the writer's intent, which may depend on the original focus of the premise. Also, previous sentence constructions would be a factor: a variety of sentence structure is important to keep the reader engaged. Too many subordinated sentences can be tiring for the reader. Include short, crisp sentences that make strong statements.

PERSUASIVE WRITING: the starting point

Method A: the announcement

The reader's interest is aroused by describing an issue or idea.

Example:

> In China today, there are over 350 million people learning English—a number that is growing exponentially.

The revelation in the above opening invites further explanation and discussion. It speaks to the overwhelming urgency for English literacy in a country that has the world's largest population.

METHOD B: the personal touch

The writer becomes the voice of authority.

Example:

> My motivation for writing *The Essential Handbook for Business Writing* came after a lengthy visit to Southeast Asia where I learned of the need for business writing literacy in multinational corporations.

This firsthand account is persuasive because the writer has, through personal experience, established credentials and an authoritative voice.

METHOD C: the revelation

In this case, there is a fact or an idea presented to stimulate the reader's curiosity.

Example:

> The weakness in English language skills of North Americans may be a direct result of an educational shift in the 1970s that essentially phased out the teaching of grammar.

The writer has presented an idea for the reader to ponder. While this assertion may or may not be true, it is certainly worthy of conjecture. Statistics and further supportive evidence would follow.

METHOD D: the authoritative quotation

Example:

> Levitt and Dubner, co-authors of *Freakanomics*, stated: "There are now more nonnative English speakers than native English speakers."

With this method, the focus is on the person being quoted and not on the writer of the persuasive message; thus, a level of credibility is created before building the argument.

PERSUASIVE WRITING: the ending

The ending of a persuasive message should refer to the main idea, but not repeat it verbatim. Avoid clunky phrases such as *in conclusion* or *therefore it is clear that*. A tired conclusion or final thought weakens the established argument. Think of the conclusion as an opportunity to reinforce the main premise.

Method A: boxing

If, for example, the argument begins with a quotation or a personal story, and closes with the same, the argument is *boxed*. This is effective because it draws its strength from the proven idea developed throughout the persuasive message.

Method B: new development or direction

With this method the conclusion extends the main premise introducing an additional idea. For example, if the premise is the need for English language proficiency in Southeast Asia, the conclusion might then suggest that there is also a similar need in native English-speaking countries. Thus, the premise becomes expanded, but a major shift to an entirely different subject or premise must be avoided.

The Concluding Statement

It is important that the concluding statement has impact. However, keep it brief and meaningful, and avoid offering a watered-down version of the points of argument previously established.

In a sales letter, the closing might be one of the following:

1. a call to action
2. an irrefutable claim that supports the main premise
3. a quotation that keeps the reading thinking long after the persuasive message has been read

NOTE: In a lengthy, formal proposal the best closing might be a list of the main points of argument. This makes it easy for the reader to review the many persuasive ideas given in the proof portion of the proposal.

SAMPLE PERSUASIVE LETTER

bold heading
sets up the
premise

EXCELLENCE IN BUSINESS WRITING IS GOOD FOR BUSINESS

Every piece of written communication that leaves a
company acts as a corporate ambassador. Improper
communication can cause confusion, may result in
misleading information, or legal consequences.
Excellent communication, however, can result in
increased business, improved client relations, and a
highly respected corporate image. It is imperative for
corporate employees to write accurately and
professionally. It is just good business.

thought-
provoking
introduction

product
introduced in
detail in a
persuasive
tone

To address the pressing need for Business English
proficiency, we proudly offer *The Essential Handbook
for Business Writing*—our comprehensive training
textbook for written business communication.
Whether an employee writes daily or periodically,
this handbook is an invaluable tool. Not only does
the handbook offer writing instructions and
samples, it is an easy-to-use reference that covers
major and minor problems encountered with
everyday written communication. Think of it as an
indispensable, self-educating instrument for
improving writing skills; think of it as personal
professional development. Improvement in writing
begins with the first use of the handbook.

strong closing
premise

To help start your staff on the road to improved
Business English writing, we will conduct a
complimentary in-house seminar on the use of the
handbook. Ongoing additional instruction is
available upon request. I look forward to providing
your company with *The Essential Handbook for
Business Writing* and to working with your staff to
achieve business writing excellence.

value-added
offer

Sincerely,

Claire Rogers

Claire Rogers
Essential Business English

THE SALES LETTER

> "Sales letters are the life blood of most companies."   *J. Venolia*

A company is always selling something whether it be a product or a service or simply its own image. The professional sales letter is so important that many companies hire professional writers or agencies to compose these letters. However, when time is of the essence, it is useful for staff members to have the skills and confidence to compose their own convincing sales letters.

+ Know the needs and motivation of the potential client.
+ Know your product and its key selling features.
+ Anticipate objections and focus on value and benefits.
+ Know the competition.

THE SALES LETTER FORMULA

Attention

First, peak the client's interest. Open with a statement of fact, a statistic, or newsworthy announcement about your product or service. Follow by indicating your in-depth knowledge of the client's business. Ask questions to show you have the client's interest in mind.

Interest

Deliver a strong sales message: outline the benefits of the product or service; offer testimonials from satisfied clients; offer sales samples or free products; suggest using the product or service for a trial period.

Desire

Indicate ways your product or service differs from similar ones. Stimulate the client by showing that the product or service you are offering creates profit, efficiency, and savings: benefits with strong appeal.

Action

Motivate the client to take the next step: to order the product, to accept a sample, to agree to a meeting, to partake in a demonstration. Be proactive. If price is a selling point, include it. If price is a deterrent, accentuate value and benefit.

A SALES LETTER THAT SELLS

Address your communication to a decision maker.

Start at the top and, if necessary, work your way down. Don't expect your sales letter to be forwarded upward to a decision maker.

Write a buying letter, not a selling letter.

Design your sales message from a buying perspective. Focus on the prospect's needs. Know why the prospect might be interested in your product or service.

Thoroughly research your potential client's business.

Conduct a thorough research of the client's company and in your letter include information that shows this preparation.

Respect that your prospect is knowledgeable.

It is likely that your prospect has researched the product or service they need including competitors' pricing. Avoid mundane facts and figures that are obvious. Anticipate poignant questions and be prepared to respond.

You will undoubtedly have competition.

Avoid reference to competitors and focus on profiling your product or service as superior. Assume the prospect already knows the competition.

Contrary to what many salespersons believe, pricing is less of an issue than value.

A well-priced product or service of excellent quality is the ultimate selling item. However, seldom is low price alone a determiner. Focus on the intrinsic value of what you are selling.

Build a relationship.

The positive, consultative tone of your communication should suggest a partnership that addresses the needs of the client.

THE SALES LETTER

> "Knowing something about your customer is just as important as knowing everything about your product."
> *H. Mackay*

HINTS:

+ Grasp the reader's attention with a strong opening sentence.
+ Use specific language to describe your product and its benefits.
+ Don't try to close the sale in the sales letter; simply create interest in moving to the next step in the sales process.
+ Offer proof of the benefits of your products or services.
+ If price is a strongpoint or if a special discount is available, highlight this.
+ Try to keep the prospect actively involved in the sales process.
+ Give the potential client a reason to consider the next step.
+ Suggest a definite course of action.
+ Initiate the delivery of a free sample; offer to conduct a presentation; arrange to send additional information. Make these offers available with a request response (fill out a requisition form, make contact by e-mail, call for a free sample, etc.).

BUT:

+ Don't overload the initial sales letter with too much information.
+ Avoid superlatives and excessively exuberant language.
+ Keep your information simple and straightforward; the prospect may know little about your product or service so include key details.
+ Avoid the use of jargon.
+ Don't use a negative approach: "*Without this product your company will fall behind your competitors.*" Stress the positive and concentrate on benefits.

SAMPLE SALES LETTER (A)

Company Letterhead

Date

Inside Address

Dear Ms. Cordoba:

A Business English Professional Development Program

With English as the "de facto" language of business worldwide, proficiency in business English has become essential for conducting global business. For this reason we have developed a comprehensive writing workshop designed to meet the communication needs of corporations such as yours.

The Essential Business English writing workshop may be of particular interest to you as the Professional Development Coordinator. We offer an affordable, effective, and stimulating professional development business writing in-service. Our mandate is to provide thorough, well-structured instruction for managers and general staff that will produce immediate results. With our proven method, participants become confident, skilled writers of business correspondence enabling them to communicate professionally in a global environment.

Our highly qualified instructors have exemplary academic and professional qualifications and extensive college-level classroom experience enabling them to offer expert instruction in writing for various business requirements.

Consider partaking in our program and giving your staff the highest level of training in business writing available. Each of your staff members attending our workshop will receive a copy of our text, *The Essential Handbook for Business Writing*—an invaluable business writing reference book. I have enclosed a complimentary copy for your perusal.

Please visit our website (essentialbusinessenglish.com) for further details and contact me at your convenience to discuss how we can be part of your professional development initiatives.

Sincerely,

Mark O'Keefe

Mark O'Keefe

Director of Marketing, Essential Business English

ANALYSIS: sample sales letter (A)

Sales letter (A) offers a service for professional development in Business English writing. The letter begins with a subject line and includes an informative fact about the global emergence of English in business writing.

The purpose of the **opening paragraph** is to grab the reader's attention: *English is the "de facto" language of business worldwide.* The connection of global business to English business writing is established.

Paragraph two addresses the reader directly and begins the sales pitch. The benefits of the service offered are explained. There is also a suggestion that the workshop ensures positive results.

Paragraph three highlights the impressive qualifications of the instructors. This is important as it lends credibility to the offer.

The **fourth paragraph** is a call to action with an offer of a sample handbook as a goodwill gesture.

The **close** mentions the website and requests future contact.

SAMPLE SALES LETTER (B)

Company Letterhead

EXCELLENCE IN BUSINESS WRITING IS GOOD FOR BUSINESS

For many, professional business writing can be a daunting task. Would an easy-to-use, comprehensive, business writing handbook be useful to your employees? Every piece of written communication that leaves your company acts as a corporate ambassador. It has been proven that inadequate communication can cause confusion or result in misleading information. Conversely, excellent communication results in increased business, improved client relations, and a highly respected corporate image. Help your employees represent your company professionally: it's good for business.

The Essential Handbook for Business Writing is the perfect desktop companion. Whether an employee writes daily or periodically, this comprehensive handbook is an invaluable tool. Not only does the handbook offer writing instructions and samples, it is an easy-to-use reference that covers major and minor problems encountered with everyday written communication. Think of it as personal professional development for your staff. Improved writing skills begin with the first use of the handbook.

Enclosed, please find a complimentary copy of the handbook for your review. I am confident that once you examine its contents you'll see its inherent value. To accommodate a bulk purchase, we are offering a 20% discount on the regular price, making providing a copy for each employee not only practical but affordable.

I look forward to providing your staff with *The Essential Handbook for Business Writing.* Please contact me at 1-416-400-8407 or at thewritinghandbook@gmail.com.

Sincerely,

Mark O'keefe

Sales Director
Essential Business English

ANALYSIS: sample sales letter (B)

Sales letter (B) opens with a headline as an introduction followed by a series of paragraphs of varying length each dealing with a specific element of the persuasive message.

The purpose of the **opening paragraph** is to involve the reader with a question, followed by the topic sentence: a message about the importance of communication excellence. The headline is reiterated at the close of the paragraph.

Paragraph two offers details about the handbook and highlights the benefits of its use. There is a strong sales-pitch closing with the assertion that writing proficiency begins with the first use of the book.

Paragraph three opens with an offer of a free copy of the handbook designed to get the potential purchaser closer to the product: they will have the actual product in hand. The discount offer for a bulk purchase is a further incentive.

The **closing paragraph** is a simple call to action.

SAMPLE SALES LETTER (C)

Company Letterhead

Date

Inside Address

Dear Ms. Singh:

ONTARIO RECREATIONAL PROPERTIES
NOW AVAILABLE FOR ADVERTISING PLACEMENT

The City of Toronto is now making ad space available in its recreational venues. This is an unprecedented advertising opportunity for your clients to reach potential customers directly. Also, your ad space purchase will support minor league hockey: an excellent public relations opportunity. Everyone wins.

Millions of families will visit their local arena this winter: a command audience for your client. Imagine potential customers viewing your client's ad for three periods of hockey. There are over 60 arenas and recreation venues available in the metropolitan area of Toronto. Should you require national coverage, we have advertising placement agreements in over 250 facilities nationwide.

Choose from the following:

    1) wall posters
    2) rink-board posters
    3) ceiling banners (custom)
    4) ice-surface imbedded ads (custom)
    5) product sampling booth placements

To celebrate this new advertising opportunity we are offering a discount of up to 40% on the posted rates. Please visit our website (xxxxxxx.com) for details or call 1-111-111-1111.
I will contact you next week to discuss this opportunity further.

Sincerely,

Sam Kaminski

Sam Kaminski
ORF Canada

ANALYSIS: sample sales letter (C)

Sales letter (C) would be written to an ad agency. The writer wants the agency to feel that they are in on the ground floor of a special opportunity for their advertising clients. Facts and statistics are used to further sell the idea. The close makes an attractive offer of a discount rate, and the writer states that he will be making follow-up contact.

NOTE: The header subject line takes the form of a press release. The intention is to give a sense of excitement to this announcement.

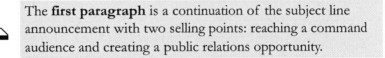

The **first paragraph** is a continuation of the subject line announcement with two selling points: reaching a command audience and creating a public relations opportunity.

To entice the reader, the **second paragraph** states a viewership statistic and mentions the number of facilities in Toronto and nationwide. The availability of a national ad campaign anticipates a potential objection (the limitation of local coverage only) and adds value to the offer.

The **list** states the standard display ad sizes with a mention that custom design is available. another possible objection overcome.

The **closing** states an attractive discount offer to encourage the reader to take action, or at least inquire further. Note that the writer will make contact rather than make that an option for the ad agency representative.

SAMPLE SALES LETTER (D)

Company Letterhead

Date

Inside Address

Dear Ms. Chen:

What do business and golf have in common? Everything.

Spring is coming and golf season will soon be upon us. Why not combine your next business meeting with a little recreation?

Hold your morning meeting in our fully equipped meeting facility with breakfast provided. In the afternoon, after a BBQ lunch, play nine holes of golf on our picturesque executive course.

This specially priced package includes the following:

1) meeting room rental, light breakfast, and coffee at the break

2) BBQ lunch on the patio

3) complimentary driving range and bucket of balls

4) nine holes of golf (cart included)

5) our golf course fully reserved

Come early and hit a complimentary bucket of balls.
Test your putting on our practice green.

We anticipate a great response to this corporate package and encourage you to contact us soon to reserve. Reservations are limited.

Visit us at www.valleyviewcc.com or call me directly at 1-111-111-1111. I look forward to hosting your business and golf day.

Sincerely,

David Lee

David Lee
Manager, Valleyview CC

ANALYSIS: sample sales letter (D)

Sales letter (D) opens with a question establishing a casual, friendly tone, which is in keeping with the nature of the sales offer: business followed by golf (work then recreation). For simplicity and directness, a list highlights the features of the offer. Mention of the affordable price has been strategically left near the end of the letter as an enhancement to the offer.

 Paragraph one has a light and friendly tone. A rhetorical question is asked to establish a conversational tone.

 Paragraph two is a direct suggestion of how a business and golf day might be set up and it includes mention of the services offered.

 Paragraph three is a straightforward list of services. This is useful because it is an efficient way to illustrate the attractive amenities included. At this point, the offer begins to appear too good to resist.

NOTE: There is a value-added offer to enhance the sales pitch.

 The **fourth paragraph** mentions two key points: the affordability of this offer and the obvious appeal it would have to many corporations. The intention is to create urgency.

 The **closing** is a call to action.

NOTE: The friendly, casual, upbeat tone throughout this sales letter is consistent with the nature of the service being offered—a fun day of golf.

THE LETTER OF COMPLAINT

"Complain to someone who can help you."
Yugoslav Proverb

When issuing a complaint, is a letter more effective than a phone call? Some complaints can be handled by telephone, but a phone call is intangible: there is no written proof of the complaint. Also, a complaint may have details (time, date, order number, etc.) that are needed to properly address the issue. The complaint letter is the preferred form of communication, and may precede a phone call that is best used for follow up.

HINTS:

+ Be brief and keep your letter to one page in length.
+ State clearly the issue you are complaining about; include dates, references numbers, and any other important information.
+ Request a remedy or suggest a plan of action.
+ Be polite and unaggressive, yet firm.
+ Use a professional tone. Choose words and phrases that convey that you are businesslike, unemotional, reasonable, and positive.
+ Include evidence regarding your claim: photocopies of invoices, sales receipts, and relevant correspondence.
+ Explain the urgency of the need to rectify the complaint and suggest a deadline.
+ Close with a friendly collaborative tone; give the impression that you will be part of the solution.

BUT:

+ Don't be flippant or accusatory; an aggressive attitude may put the person handling your complaint on the defensive.
+ Don't threaten legal action, especially if this is the first complaint notice. (If legal action is to follow, it will require a separate correspondence, likely by a legal department.)

RESPONSE TO A COMPLAINT

When responding to a letter of complaint it is important to act promptly and conscientiously. Think of the response to a complaint as a public relations opportunity. Also, in the interest of retaining the customer or client, it is imperative to handle the complaint efficiently and professionally. Responding to and acting upon a complaint is not a burden, it is an opportunity.

HINTS:

+ Respond promptly: express understanding, sympathy, and regret.

+ Thank the client (in advance) for his or her patience; reassert that the problem is rare and that it will be addressed immediately.

+ Reinforce that your company values the client and will do whatever is necessary to satisfy his or her request.

+ Refer to the complaint including specifics such as time, date, reference numbers, and other important details.

+ If the client is correct in the complaint, acknowledge this; if you believe the client to be in error, do not state this directly.

+ If the client is incorrect in the claim, explain why; reassure the client that issuing a complaint was the right thing to do to rectify the problem.

+ Refer to company policy to set up guidelines.

+ Outline the options for rectifying the complaint.

+ If possible, give a date by which the complaint may be resolved.

BUT:

+ Avoid reviewing all the details of the complaint—focus on the solution.

+ Don't appear reluctant to solve the issue; rather, be an enthusiastic problem solver.

+ Don't make any references to legal liability.

SAMPLE LETTER OF COMPLAINT

Company Letterhead

To: David Willis, Service Manager, ABC Copiers
From: Sharon Winters, ENO Systems
Date: August 12, 2012
Subject: Dysfunctional Photocopier

Dear Mr. Willis:

I am writing to request a full refund for the photocopier (model 2436) purchased June 15, 2012. Yesterday, for the third time in the last three months, the photocopier broke down, and this occurred right in the middle of an important copying session. You were quick to send out a service representative and after she worked on it for two hours, she ensured us that it was now functioning properly. Today it has broken down again, and once more we are terribly inconvenienced. Continuing to repair this faulty machine is time consuming and, frankly, futile. I'm afraid we must immediately replace this machine with a competitive brand that is dependable. Currently we are functioning with only one copier.

We have been satisfied with your products in the past and understand that this problem may be unusual. However, we cannot be further inconvenienced. We are confident that you will issue a refund at your earliest opportunity.

There is one other option. We would consider a replacement copier, but only if it is a superior model at no extra charge and is delivered within two days. If this is not an option, we respectfully request a full refund. You can arrange to have the existing copier picked up at your convenience.

Please get back to me by the end of the day with your intentions. We will not purchase a new machine until I hear from you regarding a possible replacement.

Sincerely,

Sharon Winters
Sharon Winters
ENO Systems

ANALYSIS: sample letter of complaint

This letter of complaint combines the formats of a letter and a memorandum. The text is justified and in block form. There is a salutation and a complimentary closing.

At first, the tone of this complaint letter conveys disappointment and frustration, but also determination and decisiveness. However, instead of simply demanding a refund, the writer suggests an alternative that would be mutually beneficial. While a refund was demanded in the opening paragraph, it becomes clear that the writer is open to another solution.

The **first paragraph** makes the case clear. First, it bluntly states a request for a refund; then, it offers proof of the faulty copier. This direct approach is obviously intended to spark an immediate response.

There is a shift in tone in the **second paragraph**. The writer mentions being satisfied with past service, but goes on to say that the current problem needs to be solved immediately.

The **third paragraph** takes the main idea of the second paragraph further by suggesting a mutually beneficial solution.

The **final paragraph** reinforces the urgency of the situation by requesting a same-day response. A solution is possible as a new machine will not be purchased from a rival company until there is a response to this request.

SAMPLE RESPONSE TO A COMPLAINT

Company Letterhead

August 13, 2012

Subject: Faulty Photocopier

Dear Ms. Winters:

Please accept my apology for the problems you've been having with the 2436 photocopier. This has been one of our most reliable machines so we are particularly disappointed by the report of this poor performance. You are a valued customer of long standing and we are prepared to do whatever is necessary to rectify this problem to your satisfaction.

I have spoken to our head of Customer Service, Ms. Gerrard, and she has suggested offering you two options to solve this problem quickly. We will happily issue a full refund as you requested; however, to better meet your immediate needs, we are offering to install our newest model, the 3800, at no extra cost. This cutting-edge photocopier creates brilliant copies and has many new features that will meet all your copying requirements. Also, it is a low-maintenance, highly stable machine.

If the installation of the 3800 replacement copier presents a suitable solution, we can have it delivered and set up within 24 hours. Please note that your existing service contract will remain the same.

I hope this offer presents a suitable solution to this problem. Please contact me at your first convenience with your decision.

Respectfully yours,

Jason Willis

Jason Willis
Manager, Customer Service
Direct Line: 1-111-111-1111

ANALYSIS: response to a complaint

This response letter is designed to keep the customer happy and protect the business relationship. The tone is sympathetic and apologetic, but also demonstrative. There is an attractive replacement offer at no extra cost: a huge benefit to the customer. Not only has the customer's complaint been addressed, the service provider has promoted a new machine.

The **first** order of business here is to offer an apology. It is imperative to reassure the customer that the problem will be solved. The respondent is sympathetic to the customer's disappointment, but does not offer excuses. Retaining the customer is the priority.

The **second paragraph** is the most important as it indicates that action has already been taken. The offer of two options is generous and designed to resolve the complaint immediately. The replacement computer is a conciliatory offer providing an immediate solution.

The **third paragraph** is a pledge for action: service within 24 hours with no change in contract.

The **closing** is a call for action. Note that a direct-line phone number is included in the closing, which further suggests immediate action.

ANNOUNCEMENT AND INVITATION LETTERS

Although in most business correspondence e-mail format will suffice, business announcements are best sent in hard copy. The formal business letter of announcement serves three purposes:

1) It adds formality to the announcement.

2) The recipient has a record of the details of the announcement.

3) It shows that the sender has made an extra effort to deliver this important information in a special format.

The formal invitation generally falls into two categories: business and social. For example, an opening of a new business or branch office or an invitation to a company golf tournament should be issued on standard card stock inserted in envelopes ranging from sizes A2 to A7.

Announcing a promotion or a change in staff to associates outside the company would take the form of a standard business letter sent in a #10 envelope. There are, however, internal announcements such as the birth of a baby, a staff member taking a sabbatical, or an employee promotion that are best sent by internal memorandum.

A press release going out to radio, newspapers, and television stations has a specific format (see pages 116–119). A press release may be forwarded by e-mail, standard mail, or both.

HINTS:

✦ When announcing a meeting or event, include all details (date, time, place, and directions with a map); also include the purpose of the event and the name of the host.

✦ Formal announcements should be in black print on off-white paper preferably card stock.

✦ When issuing an invitation to a business event, use standard business letter format.

✦ An invitation to a social event may be issued on heavy stock card format sent in an envelope (A2 to A7).

SAMPLE ANNOUNCEMENT / INVITATION

ABC Inc.

Annual Charity Golf Tournament

AN INVITATION

heading in contrasting font

> Join us for our 12th annual
> Charity Golf Tournament
> in support of Glenwood Hospital

tournament details and sales pitch

Arrange your corporate foursome and enjoy a fun day of golf with breakfast, lunch, dinner, prizes, and our exciting silent auction.
All in support of Glenwood Hospital.

attractive image divides document

Meet the challenge of the beautiful PGA National West Palm Beach, Florida.

Saturday, August 24, 2013

(Shotgun Start 10:00 a.m.)

FOR DETAILS VISIT: www.abcincgolf.org

TO BOOK YOUR FOURSOME

contact

David Stevens

1-111-111-1111   d_stevens@abcincgolf.org

* single entrants will be arranged into foursomes.

date, time and contact information

NOTE: This invitation has a visually pleasing design with clear and concise basic information. It should be printed on card stock.

SAMPLE INVITATION LETTER

February 10, 2012

Ms. Elizabeth Wong
Director, Human Resources
ABC International Inc.
2255B Queen St. E., Suite 218
Toronto, ON, Canada M4E 1G3

Dear Ms. Wong:

writer identifies self and states purpose of the letter

As director of student placement at FIFA College, it is my pleasure to invite you to address our graduating class at our closing ceremony on June 12, 2012.

writer describes college and attempts to persuade

FIFA College is a small community college in Ottawa that focuses on technical training, particularly in the IT field. Our graduating class of more than 300 students will soon be seeking full-time employment in a variety of technical fields. As an expert in Human Resources, any insights or direction you offer on this important evening would be most valuable to our graduates.

two strong reasons why the invitee should accept

I heard you speak at a human resources conference in 2009 and I thought of the impact you would make addressing our graduates as they embark on their career journeys. Your lengthy experience in personnel and your engaging speaking skills would make for a timely, informative, and inspiring address.

Thank you for taking the time to consider this invitation. Should you decide to be part of our graduation ceremony, please contact me at your convenience at

call to action

a.jacovic@fifacollege.on.org. I will forward details including specifics of our allowance for transportation and accommodation.

Sincerely,

Amanda Jacovic

Amanda Jacovic
Director, Student Placement
FIFA College

THE REFUSAL LETTER

Companies frequently receive written solicitations from other businesses offering a variety of products and services. Business-to-business sales proposals should be handled tactfully. Essentially there are three possible responses:

1) Your company is not interested in the proposed service or product now, nor will it be interested in the future.

2) Your company will not be purchasing the product or service at this time, but may consider a purchase in the future.

3) Your company is interested in the product or service.

HINTS:

✦ Respond in a timely fashion.

✦ Show some interest in the proposal and refer to its contents.

✦ Be complimentary in leading to a soft refusal.

✦ Use the passive voice to be less emphatic: better to say *your proposal will not be considered at this time* (passive voice) than *we are not interested...*(active voice).

✦ Be firm in the refusal, but offer a reason for refusing.

✦ If there may be some interest in the proposal at a future time, state this and suggest a follow-up within a defined period.

✦ In the closing, be appreciative of the proposal and offer well wishes.

The following two pages offer examples of an **inappropriate** and an **appropriate** letter of refusal.

SCENARIO: A proposal is submitted by a professional group for an ongoing health and fitness in-service for company employees.

INAPPROPRIATE LETTER OF REFUSAL

Company Letterhead

Date

Inside Address

Dear Ms. Lewis:

blunt opening without a positive comment

I have reviewed you proposal offering an ongoing health and fitness in-service for our employees.

abrupt tone with active voice

I regret to inform you that we have not budgeted for such an expenditure, and I do not see a change in our budget restraints any time soon.

negative implications and defensive tone

The information on fitness in the workplace you provided was informative, but issues such as liability, insurance, and scheduling would be problematic for us. Let me assure you that at present we do what we can to ensure the health and well being of our employees.

polite closing; no mention of future contact

Thank you again for taking the time to prepare your proposal. We wish you all the best in your business pursuits.

Sincerely,

Rita Mathews

Rita Mathews
Director, Personnel

NOTE: This refusal letter is blunt and the tone negative and defensive. The active voice is harsh: the opening two sentences begin with "I" further accentuating the active voice.

APPROPRIATE LETTER OF REFUSAL

Company Letterhead

Date

Inside Address

Dear Ms. Lewis:

Thank you for forwarding your proposal for an ongoing health and fitness in-service for our employees. The statistics you provided on the productivity of healthy, physically fit employees were most informative.

expresses interest in the proposal

The service you offer appears well structured and carefully thought out, and the qualifications of your professional team are impressive. Management agrees that the health of employees is a priority. However, new initiatives have been put on hold due to budget restraints. In the future, when budgets are reassessed, we would be happy to revisit your proposal.

offers compliment leading to soft refusal

passive voice is effective

Thank you again for your proposal submission. We will keep it on file and contact you should there be future interest in your offer.

expresses possible future interest

We wish you all the best in your business pursuits.

Sincerely,

Rita Mathews

Rita Mathews
Director, Personnel

NOTE: The tone of the refusal is pleasant and positive throughout the letter, but at the same time the refusal is firm. The passive voice is appropriately gentle avoiding a harsh statement of refusal.

> *"Always put a high value on spontaneous kindness."*
> *Samuel Johnson*

THE LETTER OF APPRECIATION

When should a letter of appreciation be sent?

The power of a letter of appreciation cannot be overstated. It is much more effective than a mere verbal expression of thanks. Not only does a letter express appreciation, it also solidifies a relationship. A letter of appreciation should be sent to anyone who provided excellent service or who extended a courtesy or act of kindness.

What is the best format for a letter of appreciation?

For a simple thank-you, a handwritten message will suffice. However, if your handwriting is hard to read, type the letter. A hardcopy sent by standard mail is preferred over an e-mail as it adds a level of importance to the message.

Other than the intended recipient, who else should receive a copy?

Send a copy of your appreciation letter to the recipient's supervisor. Someone who has provided exemplary service or gone out of their way to assist you deserves recognition. A letter of appreciation placed in one's personnel file makes an impact.

Are cards and gifts appropriate to express appreciation?

Cards and gifts to customers, suppliers, and business associates, especially during the holiday season, are standard practice. However, a letter of appreciation should be written immediately in response to a kindness or exemplary service.

HINTS:

+ State upfront the reason for your appreciation.
+ Focus on the reader, not the writer: minimize the use of *I*.
+ Give the specific reason for your letter of appreciation.
+ Close with a warm thanks and, where appropriate, solidify the relationship with a further thought to future dealings.

SAMPLE LETTER OF APPRECIATION

Below is a letter of appreciation written to a person who was a guest speaker at a graduation ceremony (See p. 98).

Company Letterhead

June 15, 2012

Dear Ms. Wong:

On behalf of FIFA College and the Class of 2012, I would like to thank you for addressing our students at our graduation ceremony.

Your eloquent address was both inspiring and highly relevant. Not only did you offer significant words of wisdom, you reminded the students that they are the future and that they should relish the opportunities ahead of them. Many students appreciated the opportunity to hear your speech.

Thank you for making our graduation ceremony a truly meaningful event. We would be delighted if you would consider addressing our future graduates in the coming years.

Sincerely,

Amanda Jacovic

Amanda Jacovic

Director, Student Placement

FIFA College

Paragraph one states the event and gives thanks.

Paragraph two gives praise and specific details of the impact that the address had on the students.

Paragraph three repeats the thank-you and suggests there be a continued relationship.

THE E-MAIL MESSAGE

> "And once sent out, a word takes wing beyond recall."
> *Horace, 65 BC*

The tone of e-mail communication is often conversational and may invite questions and answers as ongoing dialogue. However informal in tone, an e-mail must adhere to the basic rules of good writing.

Is it "e-mail" or "email"?
Technically, "e-mail" is correct as it is short for "electronic mail"; however, "email" is widely used and accepted today.

HINTS:

✦ Be brief and get to the point of the message.

✦ Include a subject line that gives the main idea of the message.

✦ A friendly opening is acceptable: *hello* or *good morning.*

✦ Avoid excessively formal language; use jargon sparingly and only when called for within a specific industry.

✦ Double check the recipient list; be careful of sending an unintended *reply to all.*

✦ Proofread before sending: once gone, it's gone.

NOTE: Before sending your e-mail message, check for the following:

The date and subject of the message should be included. ✓

The salutation is formal, but the tone is friendly. ✓

There should be single spacing between sentences and double spacing between paragraphs. ✓

The message must be grammatically correct. ✓

The complimentary close is formal, yet friendly. ✓

The message is going out only to intended recipients. ✓

SAMPLE E-MAIL LETTER

Originally, e-mail messages were somewhat informal. Today e-mail messaging has, to a large degree, replaced formal, posted business letters. Therefore, it is imperative that e-mail messages adhere to a level of formality and professionalism expected of business communication in general. As in all business writing, the message must be clear and concise.

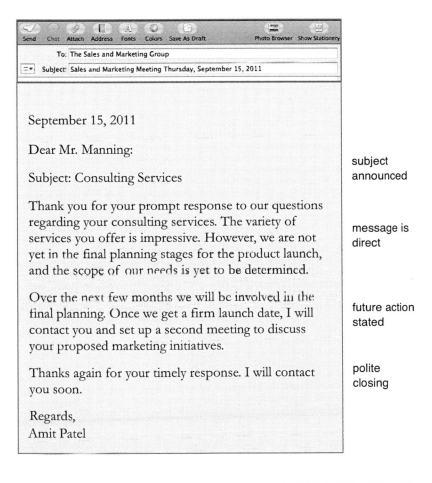

Send Chat Attach Address Fonts Colors Save As Draft Photo Browser Show Stationery	
To: The Sales and Marketing Group	
Subject: Sales and Marketing Meeting Thursday, September 15, 2011	

September 15, 2011

Dear Mr. Manning:

Subject: Consulting Services — *subject announced*

Thank you for your prompt response to our questions regarding your consulting services. The variety of services you offer is impressive. However, we are not yet in the final planning stages for the product launch, and the scope of our needs is yet to be determined. — *message is direct*

Over the next few months we will be involved in the final planning. Once we get a firm launch date, I will contact you and set up a second meeting to discuss your proposed marketing initiatives. — *future action stated*

Thanks again for your timely response. I will contact you soon. — *polite closing*

Regards,
Amit Patel

NOTE: The above e-mail message is in a three-paragraph format and includes the date and a subject line.

THE MEMORANDUM

> "Talk of nothing but business and dispatch that business quickly."   *A. Manutius*

The term "memo" is short for memorandum. The plurals are memoranda and memos, and the now popular memorandums.

The memo was originally conceived to provide short, precise, direct communication to employees within a company without using the conventional openings and closings common to a business letter.

A memorandum will state the writer, the person or group being addressed, and the date and subject of the message.

HINTS:

✦ State the purpose of your memo in the subject line.

✦ Make the subject line clear and precise.

✦ Formal salutation and complimentary close is not required.

✦ Be concise and use short, direct sentences.

✦ Try to keep the length to one page, two if necessary.

✦ Use lists, graphs, and charts as supportive material.

✦ At the close of a memo, address any anticipated objections.

✦ If required, end the memo with a call to action or a request for a response.

✦ Do not use jargon unless useful for an industry-specific message.

✦ Send a business letter instead of a memo for formal correspondence being sent outside your corporation.

THE MEMORANDUM

Primarily used internally, memos are less formal that business letters. The purpose of a memo is to pass on precise information in a simple, straightforward manner. A graph, chart, or bullet-point list may be inserted where needed. A memo may also consist of a number of sections with distinct headings that create clarity and easy comprehension.

Memos do not require a salutation or a complimentary close.

MEMORANDUM

Date: (month, day, year)
To: (person, department, all staff...)
From: (sender, department)
Subject: (captures reader's attention)

① The opening states the issues at hand.
② The body of the message gives details.
③ Details are followed by a proposal or call to action.
④ Concerns or objections are addressed at the close.

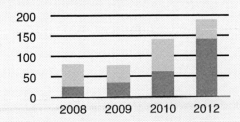

* A chart or bullet list may be inserted as support data and should be referred to in one of the paragraphs.

A complimentary close is not necessary.

Sample Internal Memorandum

— Internal Memorandum —

DATE: August 23, 2012

TO: All Staff

FROM: Paula Richards, Office Manager

SUBJECT: OFFICE RENOVATION AND RELOCATION

Renovations

Because of inadequate workspace, we have decided to make extensive office renovations. Presently, we have cramped work stations, unsuitable meeting space, and inconveniently located equipment. These inadequate working conditions will be further exacerbated by the growth in staffing anticipated over the next three years.

Relocation

The date set for our office renovations to begin is October 10, 2012; prior to that date, all staff members will have to relocate to an alternate facility. We are currently negotiating temporary space on other floors in this building. We are also attempting to secure space in the adjacent building that is accessible through the indoor passageway.

Please take care of the following before October 3:

1. Pack up or remove all personal belongings.

2. Place all old files in special file boxes available from the mailroom.

3. Save all documents on the company server.

4. Empty desks and store computers, printers, and software.

We are aware that this move will be inconvenient and time consuming, but the benefits are substantial. Once the renovations are complete, each of you will have an adequate, comfortable work station with easy access to all equipment and services.

The relocation will take place on or about October 5. Staff will not be expected to report to work on moving day.

Thank you for your cooperation.

ANALYSIS: sample internal memorandum

This sample internal memorandum is divided into five parts, each having a distinct message. The tone is conciliatory with an obvious effort to reassure employees that the company is aware of their concerns.

 The salutation is followed by a subject line introducing the message.

 In anticipation of the reluctance of employees to go through the unpleasantness of a relocation, the first section, under the heading RENOVATIONS, explains the current inadequacy of the office space and the need for renovations and temporary relocation.

 The RELOCATION section gives the date the renovations begin and states specifics about temporary office accommodations.

 The third section is informative. The use of a list makes it easy for employees to know exactly what is expected of them to facilitate the relocation.

 The fourth section in the body of the memo reinforces the benefits of the renovations. The tone here is consistent with the tone set in the first section.

 The final section gives a tentative time for relocation and states that employees are not expected to report for work on moving day—an added bonus.

SAMPLE INTERNAL MEMO (with graphs)

— INTERNAL MEMORANDUM —

DATE: December 2, 2012

TO: Sales Staff

FROM: Janice Chu, Sales Manager

SUBJECT: Year-End Sales Review

DIVISION OF INTERNATIONAL SALES: Year End 2012

Please review the following graphs
in preparation for our meeting on
December 8, 2012.

We will be focusing on two main issues:

1) Broadening our distribution channels

2) Evaluating international sales patterns

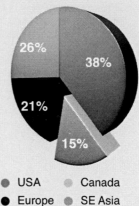

● USA   ● Canada
● Europe ● SE Asia

The bar graph compares sales by region over a four-year period.

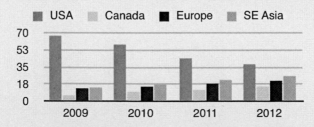

Please review the graphs and prepare to discuss sales trends. We will also
be focusing on the patterns of change with particular emphasis on new
markets: Japan, Australia, South America, and Mexico.

The meeting is on Thursday, December 8, 2012 (9:00 a.m. to 12:30 p.m.)

ANALYSIS: internal memorandum (with graphs)

Graphs replace text and save space; they give visual information that can be readily understood. Two graphs have been inserted into this memo to illustrate the effectiveness of graphic representation.

The purpose of this memorandum is twofold:

1) to inform the sales staff of an upcoming sales meeting

2) to give the sales staff information ahead of time allowing them to come to the meeting prepared to discuss the information presented in the two graphs

Note: Text wraps are used with the graphs creating a visually pleasing presentation.

The first graph is wrapped to the left by the main message. However, it is likely that the eye-catching graph will be viewed first. The title is an effective explanation of the graph.

This memo is designed to act as a catalyst for discussion. The information illustrated in the graph is not conclusive, nor does it need to be. It is enough to get the sales staff prepared for a discussion.

The bar graph is text wrapped above and below. The legend at top separates the graph from the text above.

The complementary bar graph is an extension of the data in the circle graph. It also serves as an introduction to a larger analysis, which will take place in the meeting.

The remainder of the message is inserted as a wrap below the graph. Along with a thought-provoking comment, the final part of the message informs the reader as to precise time and place of the meeting.

MEETING AGENDA AND MINUTES

THE MEETING AGENDA

Business meetings are an opportunity for live presentations in an atmosphere of collaboration. Creating a clear and inclusive meeting agenda is critical to the success of a business meeting.

AGENDA CHECKLIST

- ✓ Is the purpose (focus) of the meeting stated clearly?
- ✓ Has a list of attendees been created?
- ✓ Has a convenient time and place been arranged?
- ✓ Is the location fully equipped and comfortable?
- ✓ Has a person been designated to take the Minutes?

THE PURPOSE OF THE MEETING

Once the focus of the meeting is clear, consider the following:

1) the actions and responses of the attendees during the meeting
2) the general outcomes that are expected
3) the follow-up activities or action to be taken by attendees

THE ATTENDEES

Business meetings should be scheduled to ensure that key people can attend. People who cannot make a meeting may be able to arrange "virtual" attendance. Also, a person unable to attend may be invited to submit, in writing, concerns and opinions to be shared at the meeting.

TIME AND LOCATION

Strong consideration should be given to both the day and the time to ensure productivity. Mondays, for example, best suit meetings that plan for the week ahead; Fridays are best for meetings that reflect on the summation of a week's work. Breaks during the meeting should be planned to keep participants fresh. The location of a meeting should be convenient to the attendees and be fully equipped for presentations and discussions.

THE AGENDA

The agenda helps prepare attendees for a meeting. It should contain all the pertinent information about the meeting and should be handed out at least two days in advance.

SAMPLE MEETING AGENDA

Below is a sample of a standard agenda format that clearly states the purpose, the location, and the attendees of a meeting. The names of the attendees are sometimes replaced by their positions in the company (CEO, CFO, VP, Sales Manager, etc.). The list of presenters and the time allowed for each is useful as it gives the attendees a clear idea of the order of events and the time span.

SALES AND MARKETING MEETING AGENDA

Purpose: To discuss marketing plans for implementation in 2013.

Date: Thursday, December 8, 2012

Time: 9:00 a.m.–12:30 p.m.

Location: Meeting Room 3, 4th Floor, Head Office

Attendees: Charles Yu, Adriana Alonzo, Mark Fernandez, Susan Wang, Tara Opong, Paul Zuccaro, Anton Tchavit, Paul Edwards

Presenters:

Mark Fernandez	General Address	9:00–9:20
Charles Yu	Advertising Costs 2012	9:20–9:50
Susan Wang	Sales Forecast 2013	9:50–10:15
	Break	10:15–10:30
Paul Edwards	Staffing Needs 2013	10:30–11:00
Adriana Alonzo	New Technologies	11:00–11:30
Paul Zuccaro	Discussion Moderator	11:30–12:30

NOTE: If an agenda is distributed to attendees ahead of time, it should be accompanied by an introductory cover letter.

THE MINUTES OF A MEETING

The Minutes of a meeting should be brief, but should include the following: introductory comments, presentations, suggestions, debates, resolutions, plans of action, and details of follow-up meetings. Official minutes of a meeting may provide critical evidence in settling legal disputes.

THE PREPARATION CHECKLIST

- ✓ date, time, location of meeting
- ✓ the name of attendees and absentees (if larger than 10, name the groups or departments instead)
- ✓ the time segment of the meeting (annual, monthly, etc.)
- ✓ the topic of the meeting
- ✓ minutes from previous meetings (if applicable)
- ✓ The topic and presenter of each segment of the meeting
- ✓ motions made in the meeting: accepted, rejected, or postponed (indicate who put forth motions)
- ✓ resolutions made in the meeting: adopted, rejected, or postponed (indicate who put forth resolutions)
- ✓ summary of issues debated
- ✓ plans for future meetings
- ✓ time of adjournment

NOTE: Officially presented motions and resolutions should be recorded verbatim. And, for the record, make a list of all other statements, comments, or discussions that took place.

Keep minutes brief and easy to read. Follow a set structure and use headings for each section. Key points presented in a list make for easy reference.

Do not offer opinion about content: only report. Avoid descriptions (adjectives or adverbs) that might suggest a bias or lack of objectivity.

SAMPLE MINUTES OF A MEETING (in brief)

MINUTES OF SALES AND MARKETING MEETING

Date: December 8, 2012, 9:00 a.m.–12:30 p.m.

Location: Meeting room 3, 4th Floor, Head Office

Attendees: Charles Yu, Adriana Alonzo, Mark Fernandez, Susan Wang, Tara Opong, Paul Zuccaro, Paul Edwards.

Absentees: Anton Tchavit

At 9:00 a.m. Mark Fernandez called the meeting to order and delivered introductory comments outlining the agenda.

The following presentations took place:

— Charles Yu on Advertising Costs 2012

Mr. Yu distributed a summary of all advertising costs for the year to date. There was a brief explanation of each cost and a short question period.

— Susan Wang on the Sales Forecast 2013

Ms. Wang displayed a graph illustrating expected monthly sales figures for 2013.

— Paul Edwards on Staffing Needs 2013

Mr. Edwards displayed a bar graph indicating the highs and lows of staffing needs for the year 2013. He distributed a copy of the graph accompanied by his interpretation of the numbers featured.

— Adriana Alonzo on New Technologies

Ms. Alonzo gave each attendee a binder with details of the new technologies that will be phased in through 2013.

— Paul Zuccaro moderated a discussion period

At 12:30 p.m. Mark Fernandez called a close to the meeting with the agreement that the group would reconvene in three months to assess the progress of the initiatives put forth in the meeting.

THE PRESS RELEASE

Most companies will, on occasion, have to produce a press release to inform the public or the business community of a special announcement or important event. A company may have their own press release template or they may use the services of an outside agency. On the following pages is a press-release format outline with a sample, which would be of use to company staff member assigned the task of creating a press release.

For the media to be interested in your press release, it has to be newsworthy. To accomplish this, the writer must think like a journalist because writing a press release is essentially a journalistic enterprise. For many companies, writing a press release may rarely be required, and so it is unlikely that a company will have someone specifically dedicated to this task.

Journalists are often assigned special departments (travel, technology, etc.) and welcome press releases. However, if a press release is poorly written or uninspiring, the media may not be interested in putting it into print. Unlike most written business communication that is often solely informational, a press release requires an element of creativity to peak the interest of a broad audience. If a press release is not intended for general release to all media, choose the appropriate media group to suit the type of announcement and the intended audience.

Some press releases cultivate widespread interest because of their subject matter. A breakthrough cancer-fighting drug, the merger of major corporations, or an innovative advancement in technology may be of great interest to both the business community and the general public. Some announcements are of interest only to a specific industry or sector; however, with a little creativity, these too can be made appealing to a broader audience.

It is critical that the facts in the press release be accurate and that a "release of information" be obtained. Submitting inaccurate or false information could seriously undermine the credibility of the corporation submitting the press release.

THE PRESS RELEASE CHECKLIST

✓ Has a journalistic style been adopted: *who, what, where, when,* and *why*? If possible, these questions should be answered in the first paragraph.

✓ Is the press release *newsworthy*?

✓ Have the necessary facts been established and verified?

✓ Has the appropriate media group been selected to receive the release?

✓ Has the press release been carefully proofread?

✓ Have unnecessary adjectives and adverbs been removed, and is the copy concise, clear, and easy to read?

✓ Has a direct quotation by an authority been included?

HINTS:

✦ Choose the media to be addressed before you begin writing.

✦ Write short sentences and brief paragraphs.

✦ Use specific references for facts and figures.

✦ Avoid slang, clichés, colloquialisms, and jargon.

IMPORTANT: Just because a press release is sent out, it doesn't mean it will necessarily be of interest to a journalist. The media receive numerous press releases daily, many of which are ignored. Journalists like a press release that makes their job easier; that is, they like a compelling story with a heavy public interest slant. If, for example, the press release covers a timely topic, addresses a major public concern, unveils a groundbreaking product, or announces an important corporate merger, it will catch the attention of the media. If your announcement is of medium interest, then it is your job to compose a well-written, properly formatted press release with an angle that creates excitement.

SAMPLE PRESS RELEASE

News Release

Greenlink Publishing
2255B Queen St. East, Toronto, ON, Canada M4E 1G3

TO: All News Media

FOR: Immediate Release

CONTACT: Derek Anthony
E-mail: d.anthony@greenlinkpublishing.com
Phone: (01) 1-111-111-1111

English is now the language of business worldwide.

Toronto, Canada, March 22, 2012: Greenlink Publishing of Toronto is announcing the publication of *The Essential Handbook for Business Writing*, a text custom designed for the English-language business writer worldwide. With English now the "de facto" language of global business, the relevance of such a comprehensive handbook for the corporate sector cannot be overstated. The handbook will initially be distributed in North America and Southeast Asia.

This comprehensive writing handbook instructs business writers in the art of producing professionally written communication. John Smith from ABD School of Business states: "This indispensable handbook should be on the desk of every employee in every business worldwide." The basics of composition—grammar, punctuation, usage, and sentence structure—are presented in an easy-to-use, logical format.

John Yuen, Vice President of the International Investment Bank of Korea (IIBK) states: "Business personnel in Southeast Asia will find this handbook especially useful, particularly where English is not a first language." The book is designed to offer a lesson on every page and includes numerous samples of business correspondence that act as writing templates. Users will experience an improvement in their writing skills almost instantly.

The need for a comprehensive English-language training handbook worldwide is growing exponentially. According to Levitt and Dubner, co-authors of *Freakanomics*: "There are now more nonnative English speakers than native English speakers." The timing for the release of such a resource couldn't be better as global businesses embraces the English language.

For the business writer, in North America and abroad, *The Essential Handbook for Business Writing* is an indispensable tool designed specifically to foster excellence in professionally written communication. It will soon be available in an e-reader version.

ANALYSIS: sample press release

A press release is vital because it announces a new product, service, discovery, or business venture. This sample press release attempts to generate interest by first highlighting the emergence of English as the language of business worldwide and, subsequently, announcing a new product that is specifically designed to addresses the growing need for English business writing proficiency.

 The press release opens with a catchy header.

 The **first paragraph** states the location of the release and identifies the nature and relevance of the announcement.

 The **second paragraph** deals with two issues: 1) product description 2) endorsement. A quotation from a reputable source is inserted to add credibility and to state the benefit of the product to the business community as a whole. The tone is persuasive, yet informative.

 The **third paragraph** opens with a quotation from another reputable source reinforcing the international appeal of the handbook as a vital training resource.

 The **fourth paragraph** closes with a reiteration of the relevance of the handbook. An additional quotation is included to support the claim that English business writing is a global necessity.

 The **close** simply sums up the nature and purpose of the handbook. There is mention of an e-reader version of the text.

THE MISSION STATEMENT

A mission statement not only expresses a company's purpose, it also implies stability. It can act as a motivating force for employees and stakeholders and as a source of information for customers and business associates. A mission statement is also a form of advertising. Mission statements often appear in annual reports, newsletters, brochures, and in print and television advertising.

Generally, a mission statement is short. However, a brief mission statement is sometimes followed by a lengthy analysis of precise aspects of the company's mission.

HINTS:

+ State clearly the company's primary reason for existing.

+ Suggest both short- and long-term goals.

+ Suggest company values that are easily understood by the reader.

+ Focus on what makes this company better than others.

+ Consider who will read the statement: know your audience.

+ Know your core message.

+ Consider both the present and the future of the company.

+ Define the corporate image you want to project.

+ Create an outline and compose several drafts.

+ Collaborate with fellow employees and superiors; share your creation with others and solicit opinions and suggestions.

+ Once complete, ask yourself if your mission statement is easily refuted: be wary of unrealistic or excessively definitive statements.

BUT:

+ Avoid inflated superlatives; avoid jargon and clichés.

+ Avoid tired overused terms such as *quality, excellence, superior, meaningful,* etc.

+ Avoid platitudinal phrases such as: *above the rest, the extra mile, one of a kind.*

SAMPLE MISSION STATEMENTS

Below are mission statements from a few major international corporations. These vary in length but the premise is consistent: each corporation is making a definitive statement that best represents its product or service and its commitment to customers, clients, and business associates. (These mission statements from 2012 may have changed.)

MICROSOFT: "At Microsoft, we work to help people and businesses throughout the world realize their full potential. This is our mission. Everything we do reflects this mission and the values that make it possible."

AMAZON.COM: "Our vision is to be earth's most customer centric company; to build a place where people can come to find and discover anything they might want to buy online."

APPLE: "Apple is committed to bringing the best personal computing experience to students, educators, creative professionals and consumers around the world through its innovative hardware, software and Internet offerings."

GOOGLE: "Google's mission is to organize the world's information and make it universally accessible and useful."

YOUTUBE: "YouTube's mission is to provide fast and easy video access and the ability to share videos frequently."

FACEBOOK: "To give people the power to share and make the world more open and connected."

FORD MOTOR COMPANY: "We are a global family with a proud heritage passionately committed to providing personal mobility for people around the world."

HARLEY-DAVIDSON: "We fulfill dreams through the experience of motorcycling, by providing to motorcyclists and to the general public an expanding line of motorcycles and branded products and services in selected market segments."

NEWSLETTERS

In most companies, a newsletter is an important communication tool for making an announcement, featuring a new product or service, updating staff and clients on new developments, or simply keeping in touch regularly with associates within an industry. Newsletters are often composed in-house by managers or staff and often consist of more than one page. PDF format is standard.

Deciding on the best design depends on your message and your audience. Consider the following:

+ Is a photo or image useful to explain the main idea?
+ How can various layouts accentuate the message?
+ How many text columns make for ease of reading?
+ Which fonts best suit the message?
+ Are charts and graphs useful to explain or convey an idea?
+ What should be the balance between text and graphics?

Newsletters generally fall into two main categories:

1) **Corporate Newsletters:** these are sent to employees, clients, or members of a common group.

2) **Promotional Newsletters:** these are intended to promote or solicit business by targeting a database of potential clients, subscribers, or purchasers.

The design and content of a newsletter depends on the nature of the information and the intended audience. To be consistent, many companies create a newsletter template with logo and defined text boxes, columns, and layouts.

A newsletter announcing a new product might include a large photo or series of photos of the product. A travel newsletter, for example, might use a three-column layout with distinct text boxes and photos. A financial newsletter is often heavy on text, with the possible addition of charts or graphs to support specific information.

NOTE: Newsletters are seldom the work of one person; collaboration on research, writing, and design is normal, and sometimes involves an outside consultant.

NEWSLETTERS

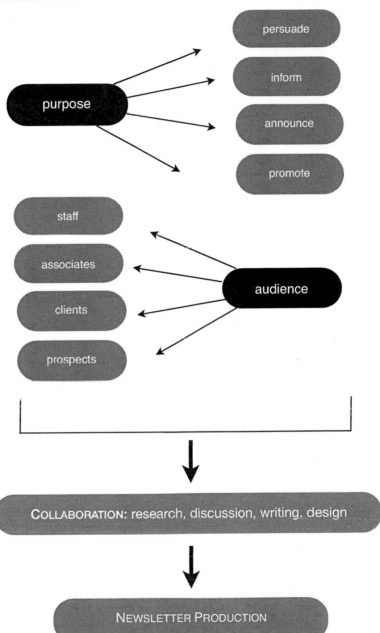

SAMPLE NEWSLETTER (A): announcing a product

Issue No. 6	Spring 2012

NEWSLETTER: ESSENTIAL BUSINESS ENGLISH

EXCELLENCE IN BUSINESS WRITING IS GOOD FOR BUSINESS

NOW AVAILABLE

THE HANDBOOK

The Essential Handbook for Business Writing offers clear, concise explanations and guidance to ensure the immediate improvement of business writing skills.

EASE OF USE

The handbook has easy to navigate sections covering principles of business writing. The text provides numerous writing samples covering various types of communication with full instruction and analyses. The basic rules of composition are included as a preliminary to the principles of business writing excellence.

With English now the "de facto" language of global business, excellence in business writing has never been more necessary.

Every piece of writing that leaves a company acts as an ambassador. Poor communication can cause confusion and misunderstanding. Excellent written communication, on the other hand, can result in increased business, solid client relations, and a strong corporate image.

International companies have a particular need for excellence in business writing. Many of their nonnative English-speaking staff in overseas offices may speak English quite well but struggle with writing in English. The handbook was devised with this group in mind.

The Essential Handbook for Business Writing is the ideal desktop companion for daily or periodic use. Essentially, there is a writing lesson on every page. Users will benefit greatly from the business letter samples, which effectively become templates for easy reference. The handbook is designed to ensure immediate results.

Features of Sample Newsletter (A): (newsletter abbreviated)
1) date, issue, and title at top with subheading
2) side banner with summary of features (Helvetica font)
2) images: logo at top left; second image breaks up text
3) two-column main text justified: Garamond font

SAMPLE NEWSLETTER (B): correspondence to a member group

TORONTO
CITIZENS
For
TRANSIT

TCT Newsletter

Spring 2012   Issue #3

TORONTO CONSIDERS A LIGHT-RAIL ALTERNATIVE

Light Rail in Toronto?

After tireless lobbying and campaigning by TCT members, Toronto City Council may revisit their intent to expand the existing subway system. Consideration for light rail as an alternative is now possible.

TCT member Ross Snetsinger, in a letter to the mayor, stated: "Comparing subways and light rail (LRT) is like comparing apples to oranges without ever having seen an orange." Snetsinger explains further that light rail passengers can see the sky, parks, and shops: they become closely connected to their city.

City Hall is adamant about building subway add-ons regardless of the evidence proving that such an extension is fiscally imprudent. A number of pro-LRT groups are preparing for a long battle with a city council that they claim is sorely lacking in vision.

TCT will gather further evidence supporting light rail and continue to lobby city council before the next council session. TCT members stay tuned: There is more to come.

Features of Sample Newsletter (B): (newsletter is abbreviated)
1) full photo to draw attention to the subject
2) newsletter title is placed in middle of page
3) four-column justified text: Helvetica titles, Garamond text

PROPOSAL AND REPORT WRITING

This Proposal & Report Writing section includes:

    1) steps for writing a proposal and a report

    2) types of proposals and reports

    3) a comparison of a proposal to a report

    4) an outline of the components of a proposal and a report

    5) a sample proposal and two samples of short reports

> NOTE: Due to space restrictions, full-length proposals and reports are not offered. Certain parts of a proposal and a report are common to both; for convenience, these have been repeated in the two respective sections.

A formal proposal may be **external** or **internal**. An internal proposal is often less formal and, in some cases, written as a memorandum. Basically, the purpose of a proposal is to persuade. The amount of detail in the proposal will vary according to its scope.

The writing of a formal report is also dependent on the scope of the subject. A corporate annual report, for example, may be over 100 pages in length and may be professionally designed and bound. On the other hand, an internal report may be a one-page memo written by an employee and distributed internally by e-mail.

If you intend to compose a detailed external formal proposal or report, it is advisable that you refer to a resource that deals specifically with formal proposals and reports.

> **This section includes examples (in brief) of the following:**
>   1) a formal proposal
>   2) a progress report (internal)
>   3) a recommendation report (internal)

A Comparison: the formal proposal and report

The following lists compare the components of a **formal proposal** to those of a **formal report**. Generally, the purpose of a proposal is to solicit business; the purpose of a report is to give information. Both a proposal and a report may be devised for internal distribution.

Proposals fall into two categories: solicited and unsolicited. A government body might put out a tender, which is a request for proposal (RFP), inviting submissions from companies vying to provide the products or services requested. An **unsolicited proposal**, because it is an attempt to garner business that hasn't been requested, would be just as thorough in content as a solicited proposal and like a sales letter, highly persuasive in tone.

Reports are as detailed as the scope of their subjects. They give information but are not intended to persuade. Recommendations may develop as a result of a report, but are not usually included. Reports are objective in message and tone.

FORMAL REPORT	FORMAL PROPOSAL
– Prefatory Section –	*– Prefatory Section –*
• title page	• title page
• table of contents	• request for proposal
• transmittal letter	• transmittal letter (for solicited proposals)
• list of illustrations	• table of contents
• executive summary	• list of illustrations
– Body Section –	• executive summary
• introduction	*– Body Section –*
• body	• introduction
• conclusions	• body
• recommendations	• closing
– Supplements –	*– Supplements –*
• references	• appendix
• appendix	
• glossary of terms	

BUSINESS PROPOSALS

STEPS

Examine previous proposals. If asked to write a formal proposal, the first thing to do is research previously written, successful proposals.

Be aware that proposals range in style. They may be written in memo format, sent by e-mail, or produced in hard copy with a formal cover and binding. A proposal may be the only opportunity to procure business or to promote change; therefore, it is critical that the proposal be properly formatted and be inclusive of all details. Anticipated objections should be addressed subtly.

Understand that proposals will vary. A proposal may be as short as a single page or be several pages long. The length is determined by the scope of the subject and the detail of the information included.

> **NOTE:** Writing a formal proposal can be a daunting task. But like all written communication, the formal proposal can be an opportunity for the author to display excellent writing skills and attention to detail. Refer to Persuasive Writing (p.72–78) and Sales Letters (p.79–89).

Proposals are written for a variety of reasons:

+ to suggest specific changes within a company
+ to solicit new business or expand current business
+ to sell a company's products or services
+ to outline procedures in a sales process
+ to provide a written record of an agreement

The motivation for writing a proposal may be as follows:
to persuade, to begin a process, to construct a plan, to initiate action.

Regardless of the type of proposal or its purpose, these three basic steps of writing should be followed:

Prewriting   Writing   Revising

THE THREE STEPS OF PROPOSAL WRITING

Prewriting

- Determine objective of the proposal.
- Specify the intended audience.
- Define the scope of the proposal.
- Develop a persuasive tone.
- Research and edit supporting data.
- Document data.

Writing

- Arrange details sequentially.
- Develop a rough plan.
- Develop a final outline.
- Write a compelling introduction.
- Devise a persuasive message.
- Write the first draft.

Revising

- Clearly state the intention.
- Present details logically.
- Be clear, concise, and persuasive.
- Verify facts.
- Proofread for errors.

THE COMPONENTS OF A FORMAL PROPOSAL (1)

A formal proposal is made up of three sections:

1) preliminary parts   2) body parts   3) supplemental parts

1) PRELIMINARY PARTS

| Title Page | The **Title Page** contains the following: title of the report; the author's name and title; the person for whom the report is prepared; the date of submission. |

| RFP Letter | The **Request for Proposal** letter (RFP) is a reference to a solicitation for a proposal by an external group. |

| Transmittal Letter | The **Transmittal Letter** is a means of convincing the reader that the proposal has merit. The quality of this letter may determine the acceptance or rejection of the proposal. |

| Table of Contents | The **Table of Contents** lists all the major sections of the proposal in the order they appear. Place the list of illustrations, graphs, and charts under a separate heading directly below the Table of Contents. |

| Executive Summary | The **Executive Summary** is essentially a synopsis of the proposal itself. In some cases this summary may be read instead of the full proposal; therefore, it should be detailed and include visuals as needed. |

THE COMPONENTS OF A FORMAL PROPOSAL (2)

The **body** of a proposal is made up of the three sections listed below. Since proposals are effectively sales letters, each section plays an integral part in developing a persuasive tone.

2) BODY PARTS

Introduction

The **Introduction** gives the purpose, scope, and importance of the proposal, and outlines the details.

Body

The **Body** section is the heart of the proposal. Because this section may be lengthy, it is useful to use headings and subheadings. Charts, graphs, and other visuals would also be included here.

Close

The **Close** offers a synopsis of the proposal reiterating key points that continue to persuade the reader. It is important that the benefits of the proposal be highlighted here.

NOTE: It is not necessary to include recommendations. The closing of a formal proposal should be reserved for a final persuasive push.

THE COMPONENTS OF A FORMAL PROPOSAL (3)

The **Supplementary Parts** of a proposal are designed to support its contents. Common parts of a Supplementary Section include: bibliography, footnotes, endnotes, appendices, and a glossary of terms. An index—an alphabetical list of the major topics and subtopics—may be included to assist the reader to find information quickly or to return to previously read sections.

3) SUPPLEMENTAL PARTS

References

The **References** (Works Cited) section is a bibliography of sources referenced. It generally includes only those sources directly or indirectly referred to in the proposal.

Appendix

The **Appendix** contains additional information not mentioned in the proposal. Surveys, questionnaires, cover letters, and forms may be included in this section. A list of appendix items is usually found at the bottom of the Contents page.

Glossary

The **Glossary** contains definitions of terms found in the proposal. This is useful for readers who may not be familiar with industry-specific terms.

SAMPLE PROPOSAL TITLE PAGE

(The following proposal is an abbreviated sample.)

ESSENTIAL BUSINESS ENGLISH BUSINESS EXPANSION	title of document
PREPARED FOR Sharma Patek Vice-President of Marketing Greenlink Consulting	name, title, and group receiving report
PREPARED BY Yolanda Schultz Director of Sales Essential Business English	name, title, and group composing the report
February 28, 2012	publication date for future reference

SAMPLE PROPOSAL CONTENTS PAGE

ESSENTIAL BUSINESS ENGLISH
BUSINESS EXPANSION
February 2012

TABLE OF CONTENTS

NOTE: The proposal and reports given as samples are fictitious and serve only to illustrate format and content style.

SAMPLE EXECUTIVE SUMMARY

EXECUTIVE SUMMARY

This proposal examines the feasibility of expanding the distribution of *The Essential Handbook for Business Writing* and the development of complementary products to markets in Southeast Asia. It also outlines the various target markets and the financial benefits of such expansion.

states purpose

RESEARCH TO DATE

subheading

In June 2011, an initial study of the Southeast Asian region was completed to ascertain the following:

1) The nonnative English-speaking population of Southeast Asian countries

2) The English-language proficiency in these regions

3) The need for Business English training in multinational corporations in major cities of this region

key points from body section

4) Countries and cities as initial target markets

5) Colleges and Universities in Southeast Asia

6) The cost of expansion throughout Southeast Asia

POPULATION OF SOUTHEAST ASIA

There are 10 countries including 11 major cities being considered for expansion in this region with a total population over 523 million. In addition, there are hundreds of multinational corporations active in this region that would represent a direct market. There are close to 1,000 post-secondary educational institutions where *The Essential Handbook for Business Writing* would be marketed as a textbook.

BUSINESS REVENUE POTENTIAL

Considering the size of the market and the need for our products and services in both the corporate and education markets, it is estimated that revenues from this region could reach up to five million dollars (US) within a three-year period.

persuasive message

To achieve these revenues, it is necessary to procure investment capital and to establish a sufficiently staffed base of operations in Southeast Asia. Subsequently, a full-blown marketing campaign should be devised to target this region. The timing for such expansion is in keeping with the growing worldwide demand for English writing proficiency.

creates urgency

SAMPLE PROPOSAL INTRODUCTION

ESSENTIAL BUSINESS ENGLISH
BUSINESS EXPANSION

INTRODUCTION

states need
for action

Essential Business English developed *The Essential Handbook for Business Writing* to address the need for excellence in business writing in the North American workplace. To increase revenue through expansion, there are additional markets in Southeast Asia to consider as well as ancillary products for all markets.

gives details
from body
of proposal

Southeast Asia, with an approximate population of 523 million, will be the focus of the expansion initiatives. Multinational corporations and post-secondary education institutions in this region will be prime markets. Developing strategies for expansion in these market segments is an immediate priority.

ancillary
products

Besides expanding our market, we intend to expand our product line. Ancillary products and services such as an online workbook, in-house training programs for corporate clients, a tablet App, and an e-reader version of the text would create additional revenue streams. Because these new products do not require a distinct market, they can be woven into the current marketing initiatives for our flagship product, *The Essential Handbook for Business Writing*.

states
purpose
of proposal

The purpose of this proposal is to address opportunity for business expansion throughout Southeast Asia and to outline the development of a complementary product line.

NOTE: this introduction is purposely brief and serves as an illustration only.

SAMPLE LETTER OF TRANSMITTAL

Company Letterhead

Date

Inside Address

Dear Ms. Patek:

Please accept this business proposal in response to the RFP submitted by you on behalf of Greenlink Consulting for the marketing expansion of *The Essential Handbook for Business Writing*. We feel that this proposal addresses key issues regarding business expansion and explores potentially lucrative markets throughout Southeast Asia.

> introduces proposal and states the authority behind it

Specifically, this proposal addresses three issues:

1) Expansion into new markets throughout SE Asia
2) Possible marketing strategies to suit expansion
3) Development of ancillary products and services

> a list is used to give specific issues in the proposal

To date, we have been pleased with the marketing and distribution of *The Essential Handbook for Business Writing*. The conventional methods you have employed thus far have proved effective in bringing the book to the North American market. This proposal has been drafted to meet the new and exciting opportunities for market expansion into Southeast Asia.

> gives specifics of the proposal

We appreciate your request that we look into business expansion and subsequently develop a proposal. On behalf of Essential Business English, I look forward to meeting with you to discuss the potential of expansion into Southeast Asia.

> offers a thank you and suggests a future meeting

Sincerely,

Yolanda Schultz
Yolanda Schultz
Director of Marketing
Essential Business English

SAMPLE PROPOSAL BODY TEXT (1)

CURRENT DISTRIBUTION

At present, the distribution channels for *The Essential Handbook for Business Writing* are limited to North American markets.

PROBLEM

states current status and problem

To date, only one market is being tapped for the sale of *The Essential Handbook for Business Writing,* and this revenue stream is limited. We have identified two large, untapped markets that should be pursued aggressively.

NEW MARKETS: SOUTHEAST ASIA

The chart below shows the population distribution for nine countries in Southeast Asia.

POPULATION BY COUNTRY

graph inserted as visual aid and to give information

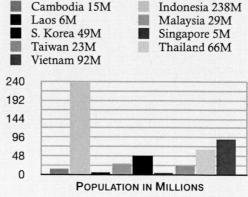

Cambodia 15M Indonesia 238M
Laos 6M Malaysia 29M
S. Korea 49M Singapore 5M
Taiwan 23M Thailand 66M
Vietnam 92M

POPULATION IN MILLIONS

Total population of SE Asia (as above): 523 M

additional statistics

COMPARATIVE MARKETS (2011)
NORTH AMERICA: **355 MILLION**
INDIA: **1.2 BILLION**
CHINA: **1.25 BILLION**

SAMPLE PROPOSAL BODY TEXT (2)

Southeast Asia is home to hundreds of multinational
corporations. Employees in these corporations fall into two
categories:

1) native English speaking

2) nonnative English speaking

explains the
market

While both of these groups would benefit from using *The
Essential Handbook for Business Writing*, the nonnative
English-speaking group may have a more immediate need
for formal Business English writing instruction.

POPULATION OF TARGET CITIES

(Total: 89 Million)

Bangkok	7M		Hanoi	6M
Ho Chi Minh City	7M		Hong Kong	7M
Jakarta	10M		Phon Phen	2M
Seoul	11M		Singapore	6M
Taipei	3M		Shanghai	18M
Beijing	12M			

list
defines
graph

POPULATION IN MILLIONS

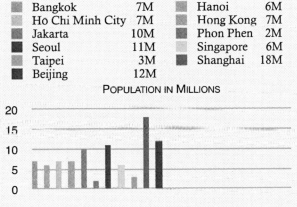

graph offers
visual
comparison

These major cities are home to numerous multinational
corporations. Singapore, for example, is a hub for global
insurance and international banking. Since English is now
acknowledged as the language of business worldwide, it is
vital that corporations train their management and staff to
be proficient in English business writing.

reinforcement
of persuasive
message

SAMPLE PROPOSAL BODY TEXT (3)

introduces new
products

DEVELOPMENT OF ANCILLARY PRODUCTS

At present, *The Essential Handbook for Business Writing* is a stand-alone product. The addition of ancillary products will do the following:

1) Support the existing product (the handbook).

simplifies
by using lists

2) Create new revenue streams.
3) Change the offering from simply a handbook to a full-service, wider-ranging product line.

Ancillary products will include the following:

1) Online business writing skills workshop
2) An e-reader version of the handbook
3 An App version of the text for tablets

SOLUTIONS: NEW MARKET STRATEGIES

recommendations

To reach the aforementioned new markets would require an increase in staff and a financial investment from Greenlink Consulting. We are prepared to enter into a joint venture arrangement whereby costs and revenues associated with this proposed expansion are shared equally.

MARKETING INITIATIVES

The first step is to perform a test market for each of the major channels: corporate and educational. The marketing initiatives below represent a significant expansion in the development and distribution of Essential Business English products.

Initial marketing steps for business expansion:

1) Build contact lists of corporations and educational institutions.

2) Contact distributors throughout Southeast Asia.

3) Create e-mail database for solicitation.

4) Create brochure and PDF.

initiatives are
listed for
easy review

5) Develop materials for ancillary products.

6) Convert websites as retail outlets.

SAMPLE PROPOSAL BODY TEXT (4)

CONCLUSIONS

Greenlink Consulting is currently the sole marketer and distributor of *The Essential Handbook for Business Writing*. To date, conventional marketing has been the single avenue for sales and distribution of the handbook. While the results of this marketing program have been acceptable, untapped markets exist that could create new revenue streams.

summary of purpose

The Southeast Asian market presents an opportunity for substantial growth. There are currently over 120 million Southeast Asians actively learning English. There are 89 million urban dwellers in targeted Southeast Asian cities, many working in multinational corporations—all of whom could benefit from using *The Essential Handbook for Business Writing*. The expansion of distribution coupled with the development of ancillary products and services would provide Essential Business English with a broader revenue base.

In a joint venture, Essential Business English and Greenlink Consulting would share the expense of establishing new markets for *The Essential Handbook for Business Writing*. In addition, Essential Business English would develop ancillary products and services to support these initiatives.

RECOMMENDATIONS

1. Develop a structure for a joint venture.
2. Establish a separate marketing group to focus on marketing initiatives throughout Southeast Asia.

uses list with strong verb beginnings

3. Assign a development group for ancillary products.
4. Establish new marketing initiatives for the expansion of Essential Business English products and services.
5. Outline a budget and a timeline for implementation of new initiatives.

BUSINESS REPORTS

STEPS

Examine previous reports. If asked to write a formal report, the first thing to do is examine the content and format of your company's previously written reports. Since these reports have been accepted by management, they will provide a proper blueprint or template.

Be aware that reports range in style. Reports may be in memo format, sent by e-mail, or produced in hard copy with a formal cover and binding. Annual reports, for example, are often professionally designed, bound, and printed. Besides giving important information, annual reports present a corporate image and should be attractive and professional looking.

Understand that reports will vary. A report may be as short as a single page or as long as 100 or more pages. The length is determined by the scope of the subject and the detail of the information included.

> **NOTE:** Writing a formal report can be a daunting task. But like all written communication, the formal report can be an opportunity for the author to display excellent writing skills and attention to detail.

Reports are written for a variety of reasons:
+ to indicate areas of concern within a company
+ to prove compliance with government regulations
+ to document progress on projects or initiatives
+ to gain acceptance for proposals, plans, or new projects
+ to outline implementation of policy or procedure
+ to monitor and manage company activity
+ to explain the details of an accident or an incident
+ to guide a decision-making process

The motivation for writing a report may be as follows:
to persuade, to give information, to evaluate, to solve a problem.

Regardless of the type or the purpose of your report, you should follow the three basic steps of writing:

Prewriting   Writing   Revising

THE THREE STEPS OF REPORT WRITING

Prewriting

- Determine objective of the proposal.
- Specify the intended audience.
- Define the scope of the proposal.
- Develop a persuasive tone.
- Research and edit supporting data.
- Document the data.

Writing

- Arrange details sequentially.
- Develop a rough plan.
- Develop a final outline.
- Write a compelling introduction.
- Devise a persuasive message.
- Write the first draft.

Revising

- Clearly state the intention.
- Present details logically.
- Be clear, concise, and persuasive.
- Verify facts.
- Proofread for errors.

THE COMPONENTS OF A FORMAL REPORT (1)

A formal report is either **informational** or **analytical**. Informational reports present facts and data; analytical reports present information, analyses, and recommendations often to help management make decisions.

A formal report is made up of three sections:

1) prefatory parts   2) body parts   3)supplemental parts

1) PREFATORY PARTS

Title Page	The **Title Page** is made up of the following: title of the report; author's name and title; for whom the report is prepared; the date of the report's submission.
Table of Contents	The **Table of Contents** lists all the major sections of the report in the order they appear. Place the list of illustrations, graphs, and charts under a separate heading directly below the Table of Contents.
Transmittal Letter	The **Transmittal Letter** (acceptable in memo format) begins by outlining the main idea of the report. It highlights body content, suggests how to use the report, and expresses appreciation for the opportunity to produce the report.
Executive Summary	The **Executive Summary** is essentially a synopsis of the report itself. In some cases this summary may be read instead of the full report; therefore, it should be detailed, and may include visuals.

NOTE: Formal reports usually have a cover page featuring only the title of the report. The title page inside identifies the author and receiver.

THE COMPONENTS OF A FORMAL REPORT (2)

The **Body** of a report comprises all the details of the report. This section may include charts, graphs, and illustrations.

2) BODY PARTS

Introduction

The **Introduction** gives the purpose, scope, and importance of the report, and outlines the details.

Body

The **Body** section is the heart of the report. Because this section may be lengthy, it is useful to use headings and subheadings. Charts, graphs, and other visuals would also be included here.

Conclusion

The **Conclusion** brings the findings in the report together concisely. An informational report may end with a summary of the data; an analytical report may end with conclusions.

Recommendations

Recommendations, sometimes combined with the conclusion section, suggest specific courses of action.

THE COMPONENTS OF A FORMAL REPORT (3)

The **Supplementary Parts** of a report are designed to support the contents of the report. Common parts of a Supplementary Section include: bibliography, footnotes, endnotes, appendices, and a glossary of terms. An index—an alphabetical list of the major topics and subtopics—may be included to assist the reader in finding information quickly or in returning to previously read sections.

3) SUPPLEMENTAL PARTS

References

The **References** (Works Cited) is a bibliography of sources referenced. It generally includes only those sources directly or indirectly referred to in the report.

Appendix

The **Appendix** contains additional information not mentioned in the report. Surveys, questionnaires, cover letters, and forms may be included in this section. A list of appendix items is usually found at the bottom of the Contents page.

Glossary

The **Glossary** contains definitions of special terms used in the report. This is particularly useful for readers who may not be familiar with industry-specific terms.

MEMORANDUM REPORTS

For internal reports, memorandum format is preferred. Dividing the information into paragraphs with headings arranges ideas logically and makes the document easy to navigate.

HINTS:

+ Write a SUBJECT line to clarify the purpose of the report.
+ Compose separate paragraphs for each topic within the report.
+ Use single spacing between lines in each paragraph.
+ Use headings in bold to introduce the topic of each paragraph.
+ Consider who will read the report: know your audience.
+ State the reason for the report with proper background information.

The following pages offer two abbreviated examples of an internal report: 1) a progress report 2) a recommendation report.

A PROGRESS REPORT

A Progress Report is usually an update of some ongoing activity. First, it describes the current situation with details; then, it states specifically the work currently underway, outlines existing or foreseeable problems, and gives details of future action.

A RECOMMENDATION REPORT

A Recommendation Report is analytical in nature and may be intended, for example, to solve a problem, to create a change in strategy, or to institute a new business initiative. Based on carefully reviewed information, the report may make several recommendations.

NOTE: The reports that follow on the next two pages are intentionally brief to serve as samples only. Actual memo reports may be several pages in length.

Sample Progress Report

<table>
<tr><td></td><td>

Memorandum

DATE: March 10, 2012
TO: Leonard Yeung
FROM: Depak Chowdhury
SUBJECT: PROGRESS OF BUSINESS EXPANSION: ESSENTIAL BUSINESS ENGLISH

This report outlines progress made since our meeting on December 18, 2011.

Background

The primary undertaking was to determine a course of action and to assign responsibilities to each group member. At our meeting on December 18, 2011, we established the first of the three market segments to be tested and decided to hire an e-mail marketing consulting firm.

Progress To Date

The three markets for the expansion of *The Handbook for Business Writing* have been clearly defined and measured. The first of these has been tested with positive results. An independent e-mail marketing firm had been commissioned to manage the e-mail database and solicitation newsletters for this segment.

At this point we are ready to move to the next phase: the test marketing of the Southeast Asian market.

Problems

The group has identified three areas of concern:

1) the possible weak response to e-mail test marketing

2) the language barrier in countries where English is not a first language or is not widely spoken

3) the expense of conducting test markets

Future Work Schedule

During the next six weeks we will continue to test all market segments with emphasis on measuring e-mail database responses.

</td></tr>
</table>

Margin annotations:

memo format

introduction to report

past progress

work completed

a list clarifies issues

next main activity

SAMPLE RECOMMENDATION REPORT

MEMORANDUM

DATE: May 10, 2012

TO: Kurt Olafsson

FROM: Raina Ahmed

SUBJECT: COPYWRITING SERVICES

memo format

As requested, I am submitting this Recommendation Report for the hiring of an outside copywriting service to assist with the business expansion and new marketing initiatives for Essential Business English.

introduction to the report

BACKGROUND

In planning the new marketing strategies that have a large advertising component, the group discussed the need to hire a professional service to produce copy for our brochures, newsletters, websites, and direct-mail pieces. An experienced copywriting service would ensure the development of effective and strategic advertising.

details explaining the need for the report

PROBLEM

No group member working on this first phase of marketing felt qualified to produce the particular copywriting that this project requires.

reason for the report

FINDINGS

After meeting with several copywriting agencies, I followed the strong recommendation of a business associate and had a meeting with the head writer at RDG Copywriting, a company that provides a wide range of writing services. RDG Copywriting immediately understood our needs and offered to submit copywriting samples to match our project.

justification

CONCLUSION

Two days after meeting with RDG Copywriting, I received sample copy and a tentative work schedule including pricing. They appear to fully understand our project and our needs, and ensures that they will work closely with us on each phase of the project. Bringing RDG Copywriting on board at this juncture would give us the professional copywriting we need and allow team members to pursue their own areas of expertise.

COMMONLY CONFUSED WORDS

This section deals with commonly confused terms including homonyms (word pairs that sound the same but have different meanings). Ten common usage errors are listed below. Additional frequently confused terms are listed on pages 152–166.

TEN COMMON USAGE ERRORS

accept / except
Accept is a verb meaning to agree to receive something; *except* is a conjunction meaning *not included*.

    a) He will gladly *accept* his well-deserved bonus pay.

    b) All staff *except* management will be under review.

bad / badly
Bad is an adjective; *badly* is an adverb. *Bad* will often be used to describe a feeling; badly describes an action.

    a) He felt *bad* about missing the sales quotas.

    b) She performed *badly* in the debate.

    c) The food at the airport tasted *bad*.

    d) The airport food was *badly* prepared.

can / may
Can refers to ability; *may* refers to permission.

    a) If I have the correct information, I *can* write a report.

    b) His manager told him that he *may* take extended vacation time.

good / well
Good is an adjective; *well* is an adverb that can also be used to mean health.

    a) He gave a *good* presentation.

    b) Because she was now feeling *well*, she returned to work.

    c) Sales were going quite *well* until the second quarter.

it's / its
It's is a contraction of *it is*; *its* is a possessive pronoun.

    a) *It's* necessary to keep strict accounts of expenditures. (*it is*)

    b) The corporation took care of *its* employees. (possessive)

TEN COMMON USAGE ERRORS

less / fewer

Use *less* for quantity measurement that cannot be counted; use *fewer* for things that can be counted (units).

a) She had far *less* work to do after the holidays. (quantity)

b) There were *fewer* jobs because of the recession. (units)

c) There is *less* time to complete tasks. (quantity)

d) There are *fewer* hours to complete tasks. (units)

than / then

Than is used for comparisons; *then* denotes time of occurrence.

a) She is a more effective leader *than* I am. (comparison)

b) First they held a meeting; *then* they voted. (when)

there / their / they're

There is an adverb stating where; *their* is a possessive pronoun showing ownership; *they're* is a contraction of *they are*.

a) She placed her new desk over *there* by the window. (place)

b) The visitors had valet service park *their* cars. (possessive)

c) *They're* interested in the overseas conference. (contraction)

shall / will

Use *shall* with first person and *will* with second and third persons to indicate the future tense; reverse this to indicate determination or need. (This distinction is being ignored with growing frequency.)

a) I *shall* attend the meeting. (future)

b) They *will* attend the meeting. (future)

c) They *shall* never agree with administration. (determination)

d) We *will* overcome all obstacles and succeed. (determination)

your / you're

Your is a possessive pronoun; *you're* is a contraction of *you are*.

a) *Your* analysis of current issues was impressive. (possessive)

b) *You're* a well-respected business analyst. (contraction)

Note: ~~irregardless~~ / regardless

Irregardless is the nonstandard of *regardless*. Avoid and use *regardless*.

MORE EXAMPLES OF PROBLEMATIC USAGE

advice / advise

Advice is a noun meaning a suggestion; *advise* is a verb meaning to offer a suggestion.

   a) Her mentor gave sound *advice* regarding sales techniques. (noun)

   b) Her mentor will *advise* her when a problem arises. (verb)

affect / effect

Affect is a verb and usually means to cause a result; *effect* is a noun meaning outcome.

   a) He was not directly *affected* by the decision of the Board. (verb)

   b) Their actions had a serious *effect* on others. (noun)

allusion / illusion

An *allusion* is an indirect comparison to describe or explain; an *illusion* is a deceptive impression or false representation of an idea.

   a) The seminar speaker made a clever *allusion* to Shakespeare.

   b) Even after her poor performance, she was still under the *illusion* that she deserved a pay increase.

a lot / alot

Use only *a lot*, and avoid *alot* entirely; and, if possible, avoid both.

all ready / already

Use *all ready* to indicate being prepared; use *already* as an adverb.

   a) The lawyers were *all ready* to challenge the ruling.

   b) The legal documents were *already* filed with the courts.

alright / all right

Avoid the nonstandard term *alright*. The preferred usage is *all right*.

among / between

Use *among* with three or more persons or things; use *between* when referring to just two.

amount / number

Amount refers to quantity or mass; *number* refers to things that can be counted or listed.

   a) Record the *amount* of time by the exact *number* of hours spent.

and etc.

Use one or the other, but not both terms together: *etc.* (et cetera) means that similar items from a list will follow.

anxious / eager

Anxious is often incorrectly used in place of *eager* to state expectation or enthusiasm. *Anxious* means riddled with anxiety or distress; *eager* means enthusiastic or motivated.

    a) She was *anxious* before receiving her performance evaluation.

    b) She was *eager* to get started on a new project.

any one / anyone

Any one refers to one person in a group; *anyone* refers to any person.

    a) Is there *any one* at this meeting who cares to add an agenda item?

    b) *Anyone* can endure criticism when it is given for improvement.

anyplace

Avoid this term; use *anywhere* instead.

anyways

Avoid this term; use *anyway* instead.

beside / besides

Beside means next to; *besides* means other than.

    a) *Besides* her, there was no one sitting *beside* him.

between you and I / between you and me

Between you and me is grammatically correct: the preposition requires objective form of the pronoun.

bring / take

Bring means to deliver something to a location; *take* means to take something away from a location.

    a) Please *bring* the files to the meeting.

    b) Please *take* these files back to the accounting department.

capital / capitol

Capital refers to a city that is the head of government; *capital* also refers to money or assets; *Capitol* refers to a legislative building.

cite / sight / site

Cite is a verb meaning *to refer to*; *sight* refers to the ability to see; *site* refers to a location.

complement / compliment

Complement means to make complete or to add to; *compliment* means to flatter or to give praise. *Complimentary* refers to a free item.

a) She will *complement* her speech with a visual presentation.

b) The CEO *complimented* her on the way she dealt with clients.

c) She received a complimentary copy of the daily newspaper.

correspondence / correspondents

Correspondence refers to written communication; *correspondents* are professional communicators.

council / counsel

Council is a noun referring to a group of people formed to give advice. *Counsel* is both a verb and a noun. As a verb, to *counsel* is to give advice; as a noun, *counsel* means the advice itself or a reference to a lawyer.

a) The matter was referred to a *council* of experts for evaluation.

b) The lawyer will *counsel* his client and hope that the legal *counsel* he offers will help the court case.

c) She was *counsel* for the defense.

device / devise

A *device* is something created, such as a tool, to perform a job; *devise* is a verb meaning to plan, formulate, or invent.

discreet / discrete

To be *discreet* is to be unobtrusive or subtle thus avoiding offensiveness; *discrete* is an adjective meaning separate or distinct.

a) Politicians must be *discreet* with their political ambitions.

b) At the meeting, three *discrete* speakers made impressive points.

disinterested / uninterested

Disinterested means to be impartial or unaffected; *uninterested* means to display no interest in something.

a) The supervisor, being *disinterested* in the personal situations of the workers, treated everyone fairly.

b) Being *uninterested* in the presentation, he slept through it.

dissatisfied / unsatisfied

Dissatisfied means to be unhappy about something; *unsatisfied* means to be in need of more, and can also be used with abstract terms.

a) She was *dissatisfied* with her demotion.

b) He was *unsatisfied* with the limited resources offered to him.

elicit / illicit
Elicit is a verb meaning to seek something such as information; *illicit* refers to something illegal or unlawful.

a) Before your presentation, *elicit* information from reliable sources.

b) The accountant was engaged in the *illicit* act of embezzlement.

emigrant / immigrant
An *emigrant* is someone who leaves a country; an *immigrant* is someone who moves into a country.

every day / everyday
Every day is an adverb; *everyday* is an adjective.

a) He worked late *every day* to stay ahead of his assignments.

b) Reading Forbes with morning coffee was her everyday routine.

explicit / implicit
Use *explicit* to refer to something in precise or definite terms; use *implicit* to refer to something implied or suggested.

a) To avoid confusion, he gave *explicit* instructions for procedures.

b) He adhered to the values *implicit* in the firm's mission statement.

fair / fare
Fair can mean just or can mean to be light in complexion; *fare* refers to the price of transport.

farther / further
Farther is used with distance; *further* refers to later time or degree.

a) The *farther* he lived from the office, the longer his commute.

b) The *further* into the document he read, the more he understood.

former / latter
Former refers to the first of two; *latter* refers to the last of two. For more than two, refer to the final as the *last*.

immanent / imminent / eminent
Immanent refers to something inherent or characteristic; *imminent* means that an event will occur; *eminent* means distinguished or authoritative.

a) The *immanent* discontent of the employees is evident in their lack of productivity.

b) With the loss of market share, stock devaluation is *imminent*.

c) The *eminent* professor of economics was the guest speaker.

imply / infer

Imply means to suggest or allude to something; *infer* is a conclusive reference to something.

a) Her absence from the discussion *implied* that she wasn't interested in taking part.

b) By not inviting her to the meeting, management *inferred* that she was no longer part of the marketing team.

in / into

In refers to position; *into* denotes movement.

a) She was comfortable *in* the company of executives.

b) She moved her desk *into* the new office.

literally / literary

Literally refers to taking words in their plain, exact meaning; *literary* is an adjective referring to literature or formal writing. The term *literally* is often misused or overused.

a) The company was *literally* insolvent and sought bankruptcy protection.

b) She made a *literary* reference to Keynesian economics.

loose / lose

Loose means not tight; *lose* is a verb meaning to have lost something.

lots / lots of

Avoid both; use plenty of, much, or many.

may be / maybe

May be is a verb meaning that something could happen conditionally; *maybe* is an adverb meaning perhaps.

a) The best time to invest *may be* when stock prices drop.

b) *Maybe* investing in a soft market is too risky.

no one / no-one (nonstandard)

No one is the correct term when referring to a person.

personal / personnel

Personal is an adjective meaning one's own; *personnel* refers to employees.

a) Her reasons for absence were *personal* in nature.

b) All *personnel* will be given health coverage by the firm.

principal / principle

Principal refers to the head of a school or to something that is most important or highest ranking; p*rinciple* means a truth, ideal, doctrine, or theory. Principal is often an adjective; principle is often a noun.

a) Excessive debt may be a *principal* cause of a recession.

b) The *principle* behind Keynesian economics advocates a mixed economy with heavy private sector involvement.

quotation / quote

Quotation is a noun; *quote* is a verb.

a) "To be or not to be" is a familiar Shakespearean *quotation*.

b) To support his point, he *quoted* a leading economist.

raise / rise

Raise is a transitive verb meaning *to lift* something and takes an object; *rise* is an active verb meaning to get up as in *standing up*.

> **NOTE:** Both the past tense and past participle of *raise* is *raised*. The past tense of *rise* is *rose* and the past participle is *risen*.
> a) She raised her voice to be heard from the back of the room.
> b) When inflation rose, consumers became concerned.

stationary / stationery

Stationary means to be unmoving; *stationery* refers to writing paper.

thorough / threw / through

Thorough means complete or detailed; *threw* (past tense of *throw*) means to propel something through the air; *through* means "by means of" or to physically go in one side and out the other.

wear / were / where

Wear means to put on one's body (clothing); *were* is past tense of the verb *to be*; *where* refers to a place or location.

weather / whether

Weather refers to climate conditions; *whether* is a coordinating conjunction that is generally used with *or*.

a) *Whether or not* the company picnic will be held next week is dependent upon the *weather*.

PROBLEM USAGE: terms often confused

A

ability / capacity
Ability is the skill of being able to do something; *capacity* refers to the power to absorb or contain.

actual / actually
These terms are rarely needed: "The ~~actual~~ time is five o'clock." "He ~~actually~~ arrived today." The basic information is precise on its own.

AD / BC
Place *AD* before the year and *BC* after the year: AD 25 and 62 BC.

advice / advise
Advice is a noun; *advise* is a verb.

all alone
Use *alone*.

all that
Avoid *all that* in formal writing.

allude / refer
Allude is vague whereas *refer* is specific.

along with
Avoid.

almost never
Avoid. Use *hardly ever* or *seldom*.

also / and
Avoid using *also* in place of *and*. "She worked in marketing ~~also~~ *and* in sales."

alternate / alternative
Alternate means every other; *alternative* means another choice.

and / or
More often used in legal or official text: "Politicians *and/or* diplomats will attend the summit."

angry at (with)
Use *angry at* to refer to an occurrence; use *angry with* to refer to a person.

appreciate
Often incorrectly used to mean *understand*.
"Do you ~~appreciate~~ *understand* the severity of the situation?"

as well as
Not to be a substitute for *and*.
"They sold computers ~~as well as~~ *and* printers."

assemble together
Use only *assembled*.

a while / awhile
To use *awhile* as a noun is incorrect. "She will work in Asia for ~~awhile~~ *a while*." "She also worked *awhile* in Europe."

B

back again
Avoid. Use only *back*.
"She is *back* ~~again~~ from England."

both / alike
Both refers to two persons or things. *Both alike* is redundant. "The managers were ~~both~~ *alike* in work ethic."

both / each

"There is a cooler at ~~both~~ each end(s) of the office." One cooler cannot be at "both" ends; but there could be a cooler at "each" end, just not the same cooler.

brief / short

Brief, when referring to letters, speeches, or documents, means concise or short. *Short* is used for time and space. "She gave a *brief* speech that lasted a *short* time."

British / English

Citizens of the UK are called *British*. Citizens specifically of England are called *English*.

C

can / may

Can refers to ability; *may* refers to permission.

canvas / canvass

Canvas is cloth-like material used to make tents; *canvass* is a verb meaning to solicit or survey.

carefree / careless

Carefree means to be without care; *careless* means to be inattentive or negligent.

case of (in the)

The phrase "in the case of" is wordy. "There were fewer employees here than in ~~the case of~~ Europe."

change from (to)

A *change from* something *to* something else is correct.

cheap price

Use *low price*. The price itself is not *cheap*, but the goods may be.

climactic / climatic

Climactic refers to a climax or dramatic ending; *climatic* refers to weather conditions.

close proximity

To mean *in close proximity*, write *close to* or *near to*.

collusion / cooperation

These terms are not synonymous. *Collusion* might suggest something secretive or illegal; *cooperation* suggests a milder working relationship. "The *collusion* of investors engaging in insider trading was discovered because of the *cooperation* of private investigators."

commence / begin

Although these terms are synonymous, *commence* is too formal for general writing and should be reserved for ceremonies. Use *begin*.

communicate

Unless used as a business or formal term, use simpler terms such as *write*, *say*, or *tell*.

compare / contrast

Compare means to examine two or more things that are similar; *contrast* means to examine things that have differences. It is possible to both *compare* and *contrast* two entities assuming they have both similarities and differences.

consists of / constitutes

Consists of refers to the parts contained within something. *Constitutes* means the result of all parts together.

correspond (to / with)

Correspond to means to respond to; *correspond with* means to exchange communication with another party.

correspondent / co–respondent

A *correspondent* communicates through writing. A *co-respondent* is the third party in a divorce case.

could (of / have)

Never use *could of.* "The executives could ~~of~~ have worked harder."

could / might

Both words suggest the possibility of an action. The confusion comes when the intended meaning is that an action is possible but not actually happening. "We (could/might) go to the meeting if time allows." *Might* shows more intent.

criterion

Criterion is the singular of *criteria.* the term *criteria* is often misused as a singular form: "This *criteria* is used to assess the project." ("These criteria are...")

D

data

Technically, data is the plural of datum, but datum is seldom used. It is not uncommon to see the following singular use: "This *data* was compiled from the research."

date back (to / from)

Date back to is preferred. *Date from* is also widely used. "The information *dates back to* 1995."

deal (a good / a great)

Good deal and *great deal* should be avoided when meaning large quantity.

decorum / conduct

Decorum is a standard of behaviour. The term *conduct,* when not used as a verb, is clear when modified by an adjective: "The *poor conduct* of the group brought the meeting to a close." (The plural of *decorum* is *decorums.*)

deduce / deduct

Deduce means to reason; *deduct* means to subtract.

defective / deficient

Defective means that something is faulty; *deficient* means that something is incomplete or lacking in quantity.

delusion / illusion

Delusion is believing the false to be true; *illusion* means something false is represented as true or real.

demise

Demise is strictly a legal term. Improper: "The *demise* of his health was due to poor diet."

depend (on / upon)

Depend should be followed by *on* or *upon.* "She will *depend on* him for support." "The golf day *depends upon* the weather."

dependant / dependent

In British usage, *depedant* is the noun form and *dependent* is the adjective form. In American usage, *dependent* is used for both.

deplete / reduce

Deplete means to use up; *reduce* means to lessen in size or quantity.

differ (from / with)

A car *differs from* a scooter. You may *differ with* someone over an issue.

different (from / than)

Use different *from*.

dilemma

Do not use *dilemma* to express a choice as in "He had a *dilemma* over which airline to travel on." Reserve this term for difficult choices.

E

each (every)

Often incorrectly used with a plural pronoun. Substitute *all* or *both* to get the plural effect. "*Each* of ~~them~~ will attend." When used together they are redundant. "*Each* ~~and every one~~ of you is invited to attend."

each (other)

The problem arises with the singular or plural verb. "~~We are aware of what *each other* are thinking.~~" "*Each* of us is *aware* of what the other is thinking."

each (them, they, us)

Each can be a subject of a verb: "*Each* person will arrive early."

either / any

Either is often incorrectly used in place of *any*. "~~Either~~ *Any* of the four plans are acceptable."

elder / older

Use *elder* when referring to two specific persons or family members; use *older* to denote advanced age. "His *elder* brother was his mentor." "The *older* man was wiser."

empty / vacant

Use *empty* to denote something that contains nothing; use *vacant* to describe an unoccupied space. "The printer cartridge was *empty*." "The office was *vacant*."

endless / innumerable

Endless should not be used to suggest vast numbers. "There were ~~endless~~ *innumerable* items requiring immediate attention."

enforce / force

A rule can be *enforced* but a person must be *forced*.

ensure / insure

To make sure is to *ensure*. To *insure* is to get financial protection such as *life insurance*.

et al

Refers to people—means *and others*.

et cetera / etc.

Means *and other things* or *and so on*.

every one / everyone

Everyone is often misused for *every one*. "*Everyone* is welcome. That is, *every one* of you may attend."

F

familiar (to / with)

A person is *familiar with* something; something is *familiar to* a person. "I am *familiar with* investment regulations." "Investment regulations are *familiar to* me."

fill in / fill out

These terms are not synonymous. To *fill in* something is to complete it: "*Fill in* the blank spaces." "*Fill out* the form completely."

first / firstly

It is better to use *first, second, third,* etc. when referring to a list.

for ever / forever

For ever means for eternity (or a lifetime); *forever* means continuous. "He will *for ever* serve his country." "She is *forever* losing her office keys."

forward / forwards

Forward is both an adverb and an adjective; *forwards* is an adverb only. *Forwards* expresses specific direction. "She took a *forward* approach to the problem." (adjective) "She moved *forward* on the proposal." (adverb) "He moved the latch backwards and *forwards* until the door opened." (adverb)

H

historic / historical

Historic means well known or famous in a period of history; *historical* means in the realm of history. "The end of the war was a *historic* event." "*Gone with the Wind* is a *historical* novel."

how / that

How is not a replacement for *that*. "She explained ~~how~~ *that* she was forced to resign."

human / humane

Human refers to the *human* race; *humane* describes an act of kindness.

I

if (with when)

Redundant when used together. "~~If and~~ *When* I see her, I will speak to her." Use one or the other depending on intended meaning.

illustration / example

These terms, although synonymous, have slightly different connotations. An *illustration* may include and image or design.

immunity / impunity

Immunity means freedom from; *impunity* means to be free of punishment or penalty.

implicit / explicit

When something is *implicit* it is implied, but not plainly stated. *Explicit* refers to an exact (stand-alone) reference.

impracticable / impractical

Impracticable means to be unmanageable; *impractical* means to be unable to put into practice.

instructional / instructive

Instructional refers more to teaching, while *instructive* means informative.

in / at
When these prepositions refer to places there is confusion. For large cities use *in*. For smaller locations use *at*. "We arrived *in* Shanghai to attend a lecture *at* Shanghai University."

in excess of / more than
Do not use *in excess of* for *more than*. "The proposed cash settlement was ~~in excess of~~ *more than* the company could afford."

in my opinion
This phrase is wordy and usually unnecessary; simply state *I think*.

in spite of
The phrase is wordy; use *despite* instead.

individual / person
These words are not similar in use. An *individual* is a person of some distinction or originality.

inhibit / prohibit
Inhibit means to restrain or forbid; *prohibit* means to disallow or prevent.

insignificant / small
Insignificant means unimportant; it is not used to denote *small* as in size.

instance (where / in which)
Misused for *instance in which*. "A promotion is an instance ~~where~~ *in which* an employee is rewarded."

interesting
The term *interesting* is vague; replace with a precise word.

"The presentation was ~~interesting~~ *shocking* but *informative*."

L
late /ex–
Use *late* to refer to someone who has died; use *ex* to refer to a person no longer in a designation. "The *late* CEO has been dead for over a year." "The ex-CEO is now a consultant."

later / latter
Later refers to time; *latter* refers to the second of two things. "She arrived *later* than expected." "Faced with two choices, she chose the *latter*."

lawful / legal / legitimate
While all of these can pertain to something legal, there are usage differences. *Lawful* means allowed by law; *legal* means within the laws of a country; *legitimate* means accepted or justified.

lengthy / lengthily
Lengthy is an adjective; lengthily is the adverb form.

less / lesser
Less (adverb) is the comparative of *little* with the superlative being *least*. *Lesser* is an adjective. "The cause was of *lesser* importance that the outcome."

M
majority
Majority is often misused to mean the greater part of something. It is only used for enumeration.

moral / morale

Moral refers to ethics; *morale* means high spirits: "Letters from home increased the morale of the troops." "The *moral* of the story is that honesty is the best policy."

negligent / negligible

Negligent means to act carelessly; *negligible* means not worth caring about.

neither...nor

If both nouns are singular, the verb is also singular. "*Neither* she *nor* he attends meetings."

nominal / low

The term nominal is not a substitute for *low*. For example, a *nominal* fee is insignificant; a *low* fee is simply low.

O

of / have

Not to be used instead of *have*. "He might ~~of~~ *have* been selected."

on account of

Unnecessary with *the reason*. "*The reason* is ~~on account of~~ the change in the financial situation."

opinion (in my)

Simply state *I think*. "~~In my opinion~~ *I think* we need a new plan."

otherwise

Do not use *otherwise* for *other*. "He expected little ~~otherwise~~ *other* than to be treated fairly."

outside of

Do not add *of*. "They met *outside* ~~of~~ the office."

P

peculiarly

Do not substitute for *especially*.

per / a

Per is acceptable with measurement. "She was given a generous *per* diem allowance." More often use *a*. "They met twice ~~per~~ *a* week."

per cent

Not to be used for percentage. The term per cent follows a number.

percentage

When used to mean a portion, the term in vague: "A *percentage* of employees have been laid off." (The *percentage* could range from 0 to 100.)

perquisite / prerequisite

A *perquisite* (perk) is an extra benefit; a *prerequisite* is a required qualification.

peruse

Peruse is not synonymous with *read*. For example, to *peruse* a document is to read it thoroughly and carefully.

practice / practise

Practice is a noun; *practise* is a verb. (The US usage is *practice* for both.)

procure / secure

To *procure* is to gain as a result of effort; to *secure* is to obtain fully.

program / programme

Programme is the British and Canadian spelling of the term. (The British and Canadians use *program* when referring to computer use.)

Q

quantity / number
"A large *quantity* of money was withdrawn; he now carries a *number* of one hundred dollar bills."

query / inquiry
A *query* is a specific question; an *inquiry* may involve many questions.

R

raison d'être
Avoid. Use the term *reason*.

rare / scarce
Rare refers to things of superior quality or to things that are seldom found. *Scarce* means in short supply.

rather than
Use *than*. "He preferred to work late ~~rather~~ *than* come in early."

rational / rationale
Rational means to act sensibly; *rationale* is a theory based on logic.

re / re-
Re is short for *referring to*, and is best avoided even in commercial use. Use *re–* with words beginning with e: *re-enact, re-examine, re-elect,* etc. In most cases adding the prefix *re* forms a new word: *rebuild, recall, reform,* etc. Revert to the *re-* usage if clarity of meaning is needed: *re-cover* versus *recover, re-count* versus *recount, re-creation* versus *recreation*.

real
Like *actual, mere,* and *really, real* is often unnecessary. "He made ~~real~~ money." "He was different in *real* life." In cases such as these, rephrase the sentence.

reason why / reason because
This usage, in place of the word *that,* is redundant and wordy. "The reason ~~why~~ he was let go was *that* ~~because~~ he was incompetent."

recollect / remember
To recollect is to consciously make an effort at *recall; to remember* is less emphatic and a more natural act.

refute / deny
To refute means to prove something (an accusation) false; *to deny* means to state that something (an accusation) is false.

relation / relative
To refer to family, use *relative*. *Relation* has a broader meaning.

remit / send
Use *remit* to mean sending funds.

replace / substitute
Replace becomes ambiguous between putting something back (in place) and getting something entirely new. To *substitute* is to replace one thing for another.

reported / reputed
Reported means to announce orally or in written form. "She *reported* the third-quarter earnings." *Reputed* means to refer to *reputation*: "He was *reputed* to be the best in his field."

requirement / requisite
A *requirement* is something needed; a *requisite* is an essential quality.

S

same / similar
Same means a duplication; *similar* implies a likeness.

same (with of)
Use *same as that of.*

same (with which)
"The same presentation ~~which~~ *as that which* was given yesterday will be given again today." Better: "The presentation given yesterday will be given again today."

satisfied that
Avoid when meaning to believe. "I ~~was satisfied that~~ *believed* that the facts were accurate."

separate between
Use *distinguish between* or *separate from.*

similar / analogous
Similar means to have likeness or common characteristics. *Analogous* means to be compared by *analogy* or reasoning (*analogous to*). Use *similar to* instead of *similar as.*

simplistic / simple
Simplistic means to be overly simple and thus is derogatory; it is not a synonym for *simple,* which could be complimentary. Avoid wordiness such as *too simple* and *overly simplistic.*

sociable / social
Social refers to society, such as "social unrest"; *Sociable* means friendly or gregarious.

source / cause
Source means the root or origin of something; *cause* means the reason for something. "The ~~source~~ *cause* of his illness is unknown." "The *source* of the problem was an accounting error."

spell (spelt, spelled)
Spelt is British and Canadian usage; *spelled* is American usage.

state / say
State is a much stronger term and should be reserved for formal or emphatic use. "When I arrive I ~~state~~ *say* good morning to everyone." "She will ~~say~~ *state* the company's position on foreign investment."

supplement / complement
A *supplement* is an addition to something originally complete; a *complement* is an important second part of or addition to something.

U

unique
Unique means one of a kind and cannot be *very unique, rather unique,* or *quite unique.*

W

whether or no / not
Use *whether or not.*

wide / broad (width / breadth)
Wide suggests distance; *broad* suggests magnitude.

would best / had best
For the first person, use *had best*: "I ~~would~~ *had best* be prepared for the meeting."

VISUAL DESIGN BASICS

All documents require an element of design, which can be as simple as selecting an appealing and functional font or as detailed as creating balance and distribution on a page. The task of design may also include constructing sections with titles and subtitles and inserting graphic elements (graphs, charts, illustrations, etc.).

CREATING A DOCUMENT

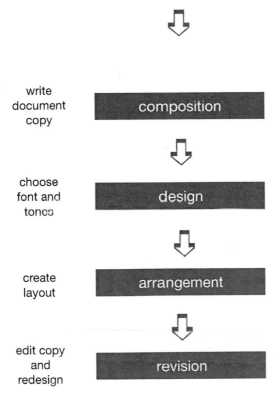

WORKING WITH FONTS

There are basically two font categories: **serif** and **sans serif**. **Serif fonts** have short extensions on the ends of the main part of the letters. With **sans serif** fonts the strokes of the letters end without serifs. In addition to these fonts, there are two font categories of lesser importance: *script* and **novelty** fonts. If a document is laden with inappropriate or inconsistent fonts, it will be hard to read and annoying to the reader.

The fonts you choose for your document should adhere to the following rules:

1) Fonts should not be distracting.
2) Fonts should be simple and easy to read.
3) Fonts should be consistent throughout the document.
4) Fonts should suit the message.

serif	sans serif	*script*	*novelty*
font	font	*font*	**font**

SIMPLE FONT USAGE RULES

+ Use serif font for main body text.
+ Use sans serif font for headings or special messages.
+ Use script font for personal messages: invitations, etc.
+ Use novelty font for short, casual messages or for advertising copy.

WORKING WITH FONTS

With hundreds of fonts to choose from, selecting the right font for a document can be difficult. Below are lists of commonly used fonts. Although all these fonts are 10 point in measurement, they differ in size. (See next page.)

serif	sans serif
Baskerville	Abadi
Bell MT	Arial
Bodoni	Bell Gothic
Book Antique	Century Gothic
Bookman Old Style	Futura
Courier New	Geneva
Garamond	Gill Sans
Georgia	Helvetica
Goudy Old Style	Lucida Sans
Hoefler	Microsoft Sans Serif
Palatino	Tahoma
Times New Roman	Verdana

NOTE: Major corporations choose the following fonts for their websites: Apple (Lucida); Amazon (Verdana); Microsoft (Tahoma); IBM (Arial); Twitter (Helvetica); Facebook (Lucida).

WORKING WITH FONTS

Although all the fonts in the chart on the previous page are 10 point, it is the difference in the x height that determines size. The x height is the height of the lower case letters.

Type size is determined by the spread from the highest to the lowest letter stroke in a word. The word *Sample* below is written in 18-point Verdana font.

type size: from top   **[Sample]**   *x* height: the size of
of *S* to bottom of *p*   lower case letters

Note the difference in size of the three samples below even though each is written in 18-point font.

Gills Sans	Bell Gothic	Century Gothic
[Sample]	**[Sample]**	**[Sample]**

HINTS:

✦ Create your own font comparison page: place a word on a page and change it to various fonts. Print out the page and compare these font samples for size and readability.

✦ Choose a font that fits into the text space.

✦ Make sure there is adequate space between lines to best display the font you choose.

✦ Not all fonts are web compatible; stay with conventional fonts.

✦ Serif fonts make body text easy to read as they create a subtle flow from letter to letter.

✦ Limit the number of fonts in your document: a heading font (**sans serif**) and a body text font (**serif**).

✦ Retain a certain amount of "white space" in your document to set off text and make the overall document easier to read.

THE IMPACT OF ART IN A DOCUMENT

Used properly, art is a creative and efficient communication tool that supports and reinforces textual information. For example, the inclusion of a chart or graph can present facts and figures readily understandable.

Adding art enhances a document in the following ways:

1) Art creates a visual communication of information.

2) Art complements textual information.

3) Art relays large amounts of information instantly.

4) Art creates eye-catching displays.

5) Art breaks up text-heavy documents.

To use art effectively, two elements must be considered: the information content and the appearance.

✦ The **information content** of an image should complement the text by clarifying or defining information and by supporting facts found in the text.

✦ The **appearance** of an image depends on its size, its shape, and its orientation on the page. Tone and contrast effect the way the reader reacts to the image. With simple photo adjustment tools, images can be altered to suit.

The merging of text and art must appear seamless. An image should blend with the text creating a logical association between the two. There are three elements to combining text and art:

1) **POSITIONING:** the image should be placed close to the corresponding text.

2) **VISUAL FIT:** the integration of the image into the text should be balanced.

3) **SIZE:** the image should be in proportion to the page.

PAGE DESIGN

Often you will be faced with important design considerations when producing a document.

Are you trying to fit your body text into a single page?

Is there a graphic element to be included?

Are there headings and subheadings?

Is there text that requires the reader's special attention?

Does placing your text in two or three columns work best?

Are there restrictions due to page size?

THREE ELEMENTS OF PAGE DESIGN

Below, basic body text is combined with three basic elements of page design: headings (display text), white space, and art (graphics).

heading

subheading

white space

text

image wrap

white space

text

English is the Language of Business

Businesses are intent on improving the English writing skills of their employees.

Malesuada quis, egestas quis, wisi. Donec ac sapien. Ut orci. Duis ultricies, metus a feugiat porttitor, dolor mauris convallis est, quis mattis lacus ligula eu augue. Sed facilisis. Morbi lorem mi, tristique vitae, sodales eget, hendrerit sed, erat lorem ipsum dolor.

Malesuada quis, egestas quis, wisi. Donec ac sapien. Ut orci. Duis ultricies, metus a feugiat porttitor, dolor mauris convallis est, quis mattis lacus ligula eu augue. Sed facilisis. Morbi lorem mi, tristique vitae, sodales eget, hendrerit sed, erat lorem ipsum dolor. Malesuada quis, egestas quis, wisi. Donec ac sapien. Ut orci. Duis ultricies, metus a feugiat porttitor, dolor mauris convallis est, quis mattis lacus ligula eu augue. Sed

Balancing Visual Elements

When a visual element is included with body text, be sure to proportion it so it does not overpower the text. In the first sample below, the left-aligned text and the image are in harmony. In the second example, the image is too large for the text and the awkward alignment makes the text difficult to read.

Lorem ipsum dolor sit amet, ligula nulla pretium, rhoncus tempor placerat fermentum, enim integer ad vestibulum volutpat. Nisl turpis est, vel elit, congue wisi enim nunc ultricies sit, magna tincidunt. Maecenas aliquam maecenas ligula nostra, accumsan taciti. Sociis mauris in integer, a dolor netus non dui aliquet, sagittis felis sodales, dolor sociis mauris, vel eu libero cras. Interdum at. Eget habitasse elementum est, ipsum purus pede porttitor class, ut, aliquet sed auctor, imperdiet arcu per diam dapibus libero duis. Enim eros in vel, volutpat nec leo,

text aligned left; image in harmony with text

NOTE: The text in the example above is aligned left; the text in the example below is wrapped, but the image is too large and overpowers the text.

Lorem ipsum dolor sit amet, ligula nulla pretium, rhoncus tempor placerat fermentum, enim integer ad vestibulum volutpat. Nisl turpis est, vel elit, congue wisi enim nunc ultricies tincidunt. aliquam ligula accumsan Sociis integer, a non dui sagittis felis sodales, dolor sociis mauris, vel eu libero nunc sit, magna Maecenas maecenas nostra, taciti. mauris in dolor netus aliquet,

image is too large and overpowers the text

EMPHASIS

Occasionally you may want to draw the reader's attention to a specific illustration, text, heading, subheading, or message. This can be accomplished several ways:

1) Establish a contrast with other elements on a page by inserting an image.

2) Increase font size or highlight with a second font.

3) Add a heading or subheading to a section.

4) Move text to the middle of the page.

5) Underline text or place it in italics.

Helvetica font
heading

subheading in
grey Helvetica

body text
justified
(Garamond)

special message
set off from
body text

body text
justified

image adds
contrast

THE ART OF DESIGN

GETTING STARTED

Lorem ipsum dolor sit amet, consectetur adipiscing elit, set eiusmod tempor incidunt et labore et dolore magna aliquam. Ut enim ad minim veniam, quis nostrud exerc. Irure dolor in reprehend incididunt ut labore et dolore magna

Follow the basic principles of design and your document will be appealing.

Lorem ipsum dolor sit amet, consectetur adipiscing elit, set eiusmod tempor incidunt et labore et dolore magna aliquam. Ut enim ad minim veniam, quis nostrud exerc. Irure dolor in reprehend incididunt ut labore et dolore magna aliqua. Ut

The
Essential
Handbook
For
Business
Writing

*communicate excellence in English,
the language of business worldwide*

Desmond A. Gilling

TEXT ALIGNMENT

Below are four text alignments to consider when presenting written material.

middle aligned

Middle text must
be strategically placed to avoid
dangling a
word on a separate
line.
(as in this case)

Middle aligned text often appears in invitations, notices, and title pages. It should be balanced with a mix of short and long lines to accent key terms such as titles, names, dates, or instructions.

justified

Justified text creates a clean, orderly look. It is an efficient way to present information, and is often used in newspapers, reports, and books.

Uneven gaps can occur making the copy look unbalanced. To avoid gaps, match up the line length with the type size. Look out for lines that are too short and words that are too long.

flush-left

Flush-left text adheres to the natural flow of reading (left to right on a page). The left edge is straight; the right edge is uneven.

Unlike justified text, flush-left text does not suffer from erratic spacing. The right edge should look natural and pleasantly uneven without excessive hyphenation.

flush-right text

Flush-right text is rarely used
and may seem awkward to
some readers. Finding the
beginning of a ragged line can
be annoying. It is best used
with short bursts of text.

Flush-right text works well with call-outs and captions placed on the left edge. Because flushed-right text is unusual, it can be a pleasant relief from ordinary layouts.

TEXT ALIGNMENT

Justified text is orderly and balanced.

Donec enim orci, ultricies in, malesuada quis, egestas quis, wisi. Donec ac sapien. Ut orci. Duis ultricies, metus a feugiat porttitor, dolor mauris convallis est, quis mattis lacus ligula eu augue. Sed facilisis. Morbi lorem mi, tristique vitae, sodales eget, hendrerit sed, erat. Vestibulum eget purus vitae eros

Flush left is natural to the reader.

Donec enim orci, ultricies in, malesuada quis, egestas quis, wisi. Donec ac sapien. Ut orci. Duis ultricies, metus a feugiat porttitor, dolor mauris convallis est, quis mattis lacus ligula eu augue. Sed facilisis. Morbi lorem mi, tristique vitae, sodales eget, hendrerit sed, erat. Vestibulum eget purus vitae eros ornare adipiscing. Vivamus nec quam.

Flush right works with callout information.

subheading

call-out

Donec enim orci, ultricies in, malesuada quis, egestas quis, wisi. Donec ac sapien. Ut orci. Duis ultricies, metus a feugiat porttitor, dolor mauris convallis est, quis mattis lacus ligula eu augue.

Middle aligned text is balanced and easy to read. Key parts of the message are on single lines.

– AN INVITATION –

All Office Staff Come Celebrate

Please join us to celebrate the promotion
of Susan Bradley to
Senior Account Executive

Date: Friday, August 17, 2012
Location: Boardroom A
Please confirm your attendance by e-mail
to Roccina Fonza by August 3, 2012.

CHARTS AND GRAPHS

THE FLOW CHART

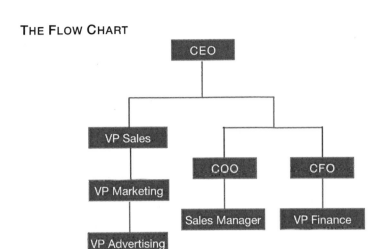

Charts and graphs are clear and simple ways to illustrate relationships. The above flow chart shows the hierarchal order of a corporate structure. Flow charts can also define the order of events in a work project. Below is a bar graph illustrating the top ten English-speaking countries in the world.

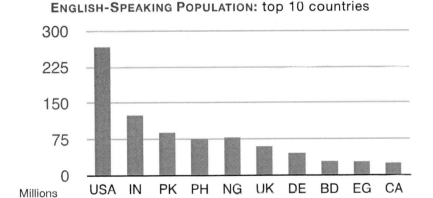

ENGLISH-SPEAKING POPULATION: top 10 countries

USA...United States
IN.......India
PK......Pakistan
PH......Philippines
NG......Nigeria

UK...United Kingdom
DE...Germany
BD...Bangladesh
EG...Egypt
CA...Canada

TABLE CHART

The table below is ideal for displaying and comparing information. A legend is included to complement the abbreviated names of the countries listed.

TOP TEN ENGLISH-SPEAKING COUNTRIES

Country	English	Eligible Pop. (millions)	Total English Speaking (millions)	English First Language (millions)	English Other Language (millions)
USA	95	281	267	226	42
IN	12	1,210	125	0.25	350
PK	49	181	89	N/A	89
PH	79	97	76	3	73
NG	53	148	79	4	75
UK	98	61	60	58	2
DE	56	82	46	0.25	46
BD	18	163	29	N/A	29
EG	35	28	28	N/A	28
CA	85	33	25	18	8

LEGEND

USA...United States
IN.......India
PK......Pakistan
PH......Philippines
NG......Nigeria

UK...United Kingdom
DE...Germany
BD...Bangladesh
EG...Egypt
CA...Canada

INDEX